Engage Your Wor

A Practical Guide to Having Spiritual Conversati...

Participant Guide

Illustrations: Heather Birkeland

Special thanks to editors Tricia Scribner and Sara Cross.

ISBN: 978-1-7358590-0-2

ENGAGE 360

The content of this 6-week small group curriculum is designed to be read and discussed in a group setting. For more information, and to access additional resources, go to www.E360m.org/eywresources.

www.E360m.org

Know The Gospel Basics

(1 Cor. 15:3-8)

	Four Gospel Points	Why They Are Important
PROVES	1. Jesus DIED	To cleanse us from sin
	2. Jesus was BURIED	Demonstrates that He died
PROVES	3. Jesus ROSE from the dead	Showed that He was the Son of God who successfully defeated death
	4. Jesus APPEARED bodily to many people	Demonstrates that He rose from the dead

My/Our Evangelism Goal

I will **know** The Gospel Basics and pray for opportunities to share my faith in everyday conversations.

I will **show** genuine love and interest for people by asking questions and meeting them on common ground.

I will **not judge** my success by how I feel or by comparison to others, but seek steady personal growth in faithful obedience to Christ.

–Matthew 28:16-20

____

(Signature)

Evangelism Survey (Beginning)

Date: ________

1	2	3	4	5
Need Practice		Making Progress		Confident/ Comfortable

How comfortable are you starting a spiritual conversation? ________

(On a scale of 1 to 5, with 5 being "Comfortable" and 1 being "Not very comfortable", write down the number.)

Once started, how comfortable are you guiding a spiritual conversation? ________

(On a scale of 1 to 5, with 5 being "Comfortable" and 1 being "Not very comfortable", write down the number.)

How confidently can you explain the Gospel to someone? ________

(On a scale of 1 to 5, with 5 being "Comfortable" and 1 being "Not very comfortable", write down the number.)

How often do you have spiritual conversations with others? (Circle the word that best describes where you are.)

Daily **Weekly** **Monthly** **Rarely** **Never**

When you finish Session 6, please fill out the follow-up survey on page 134.
Please enter results from both surveys at www.E360m.org/EYWsurvey

Table of Contents

"DYNA MO"

Christian, extrovert; wants to share faith and LOVES talking to people but is afraid of saying the wrong thing or unsure how to talk about the Gospel.

"S.K. EPTIC"

Non-Christian, skeptic extraordinaire! If you have answers, "S.K." has objections! "S.K." will definitely sharpen our responses. Maybe that skepticism is covering up a deeper hurt?

Meet Our Cast

Our cast members will help us learn how to share our faith by bringing their personalities and points of view into the conversation.

They will help us learn about ourselves, about how to have better conversations with others, how to be more understanding of others, and hopefully a little more confident in starting conversations with our co-workers, friends, family, and yes, even strangers!

"REESE ZERVE"

Christian, introvert; wants to share faith but has a hard time talking to people and would rather be with 2 or 3 close friends.

"A.G. NOSTIC"

Non-Christian; not sure about beliefs, doesn't have a church background, may have incorrect ideas about Christianity.

"CHRISTIAN PĒCĒ"

Cultural Christian; goes to church, volunteers a lot, and believes the best way to share our faith is to love each other.

"WHIRL D. VUE"

Non-Christian; sometimes plays a Muslim, Mormon, Jehovah's Witness, or other worldview we might interact with while sharing our faith.

Session 1

Sharing My Faith: Can I Do This?

Walk in wisdom toward outsiders, making the best use of the time. Let your speech always be gracious, seasoned with salt, so that you may know how you ought to answer each person.

–Colossians 4:5-6

. . .

As a Christian, have you ever walked away from a conversation and realized you had just missed an opportunity to talk about spiritual things and maybe even share the Gospel because you couldn't figure out where to begin?

If you answered "yes," then you are in good company. There are often opportunities to share our faith with friends, family, co-workers, and even strangers, but we may lack the skills or the confidence (or both) to initiate such conversations. That's where this study comes in, and the good news is that you've taken the first step toward success just by embarking on this study.

Like GPS directions, this study guides you turn-by-turn to build the knowledge and skills you can start using right now to transform your daily conversations into spiritual conversations that point people toward Jesus.

. . .

Start Where You Are

Imagine you are at work, and a new co-worker comes up to you and says, "Thanks again for taking me to lunch the other day. Our family is heading to the lake on Sunday; would your family like to join us?"

During your lunch earlier in the week the conversation never made it to spiritual topics, and you had been wondering how you could start a conversation with them about faith and spiritual matters. This might be the opportunity you have been praying for. **Are you ready?**

How would you suggest Reese Zerve respond to their co-worker?

...

The co-worker turns and begins walking away. Inside your head, an alarm goes off. This is the opportunity you've been praying for, but what should you say? One more second and it will be awkward to say anything. Just like that, the opportunity is gone. Maybe next time.

Many of us would find ourselves tongue-tied and might not know what to say or how to naturally turn the conversation to spiritual things. At Engage 360 we are convinced that God regularly gives us opportunities in our everyday lives like the example above. But sometimes we just need some help to make the most of these opportunities.

It takes practice to be ready for these interactions, and that is exactly what the next six weeks are designed to do. If you apply yourself and interact with your group, you will grow in skill and confidence for initiating and directing conversations toward spiritual matters.. But first, start by considering where you are right now in terms of concerns and confidence in having spiritual conversations.

...

Think about a time when you have been in a similar situation as Reese Zerve. How might you have responded differently? Write it down and share it with the group.

____

____

____

____

____

What concerns keep you from sharing the Gospel in daily conversations?

(Check all that apply or add your own.)

- ☐ "I'm afraid of offending someone or damaging a relationship."
- ☐ "I really don't know what to say or even how to start."
- ☐ "I really don't think about it in daily conversations."
- ☐ "I don't want to sound like a fanatic."
- ☐ "I wouldn't know how to answer questions they might ask."
- ☐ Other ______________________________

Right now, the sentence that best describes my confidence to start a spiritual conversation is...

- ☐ "No way that I could do that!"
- ☐ "I might be able to in the perfect situation."
- ☐ "I could do it, but it is very hard."
- ☐ "I can, but need improvement."
- ☐ "I do it all the time with confidence."
- ☐ Other ______________________________

Right now, the sentence that best describes my ability to guide a spiritual conversation once it is started is...

- ☐ "I freeze up and miss most opportunities."
- ☐ "I try, but don't really know what to say."
- ☐ "I can explain the Gospel and basics of Christianity, but don't know how to deal with questions."
- ☐ "I can often guide conversations towards spiritual matters, but need improvement."
- ☐ "I feel very confident, no matter what I am asked or to whom I am talking."
- ☐ Other ______________________________

...

Most of us have fears about having spiritual conversations. In fact, it is our fears that can actually motivate us to be better prepared to talk with non-Christians about spiritual matters, including the Gospel. Be encouraged! Wherever you find yourself on these self-assessment scales, you can grow and the next six weeks will help you do that.
We can also remind ourselves that we have the Holy Spirit working in us to enable all that He asks us to do. He is our teacher and our guide, and knows the desires of our heart to grow in faith and competence in sharing our faith.

Read Philippians 2:13

...

LET'S DO A *SPIRITUAL BACKGROUND CHECK!!* ASK YOURSELF THREE QUESTIONS AND ANSWER WITHOUT CONSULTING SOURCES. THIS IS FOR YOUR PERSONAL KNOWLEDGE AND GROWTH.

1. Why Are You A Christian?

Have you asked yourself why you believe in Jesus Christ? Have you ever had to explain this to someone? Discuss a time when you have explained to someone about why you are a Christian. Were you comfortable? How did it go?

(Imagine someone is standing in front of you right now and asks, "Why are you a Christian?" Write your answer below.)

2. What Are Your Motives For Sharing the Gospel?

Below are some unhealthy motives for sharing the Gospel. Have you struggled with any of these? If so, which one(s)?

- [ ] *Trying to earn points with God.*

  Legalism–Trying to earn points with God; doing something just because it's a rule and because we think that keeping the rule makes God pleased with us.

- [ ] *Feeling good about ourselves by acting like we are better than others.*

  Self-righteous Attitude–Feeling better about ourselves in comparison to other Christians when sharing the Gospel.

- [ ] *Feeling like we are obligated because the Bible says we are commanded to share the Gospel.*

  Lack of Love–Sharing the Gospel only because the Bible commands us to, and we feel obligated.

- [ ] *Wanting to look good to fellow Christians.*

  Prideful Attitude–Sharing the Gospel to impress other Christians.

Unhealthy Motives Reveal a Misunderstanding of the Gospel and the God of the Gospel

...

E360 team member Tricia once had a friend who as a new Christian was determined to share the Gospel with at least one person a day. He frequently walked up to random strangers and asked them if they knew Christ as their Savior. We appreciate his zeal, but we want to learn how to share out of more than obligation and in a way that demonstrates care for the person, not just for their response.

...

Read Romans 12:1-3

Will You Please Answer These Questions?

1. We present our bodies and lives to God as

______________________.

2. We turn from aligning ourselves with worldly thinking to being transformed by the __________ of our mind with godly right thinking.

3. Instead of thinking highly of ourselves, we humbly examine ourselves with sober

__________________________.

Here are some biblical motivations for sharing your faith. Read each passage and write down what the writer says the passage reveals as a right motive for sharing the Gospel. Write down which motivations you will focus on developing as you intentionally share your faith!

(Romans 10:1) ____

(Romans 5:6-11) ____

(Matthew 28:16-20) ____

____

3. How Do I Measure Success?

Closely related to the issue of motives is how we measure success in a spiritual conversation. The truth is, how we measure success will impact our future efforts to speak about our faith or even about any spiritual issues.

We can have mistaken views about success. When we recognize these errors in our thinking, we have taken the first step to changing and growing.

Mistake 1: Comparing ourselves with others

Tricia says that her son-in-law is a natural evangelist. "If I compared myself with him, I'd get discouraged and quit. As a kid, I couldn't even sell Girl Scout Cookies®. How could I possibly hope to be successful sharing the Gospel? But I recognize that while my son-in-law is gifted in evangelism, and I am not a good salesperson, God wants me to share in my own voice, through my own personality and story, about the gift of salvation He has personally given me."

Mistake 2: Focusing on performance

While evaluating our presentation and seeking to improve is a good thing, beating ourselves up over every verbal misstep is not helpful, and places the focus on ourselves instead of on the Lord's ability to work through every willing heart and His desire and ability to bring the lost to Him.

Mistake 3: Measuring success by how the person responds

When we long for a positive response in a conversation with a non-Christian and get nowhere, we can leave thinking, "Where did I go wrong? Maybe I'm just not good at this." When this happens, we tend to shut down and fear sharing in future conversations.

(Make a note of which of these three mistakes you are most likely to make when sharing your faith and why you think this is most likely.)

...

Let's replace the three mistakes in how we measure our success with three truths that we can tuck away in our hearts.
When you experience concern or discouragement after an attempt to initiate a spiritual conversation or share the Gospel, pull these out and review them.

...

Truth 1: You are your own measuring stick!

If you are a recreational league basketball player but measure your success against being as good as Michael Jordan, you will always fail, no matter how much you improve. Look to others for inspiration, advice, or accountability, but always remember: you are your own measuring stick! You may not think you are growing and improving, but when you look back after a few months, you will recognize that you have more love, knowledge, skills, and confidence. In short, you are making steady improvement in your willingness and ability to share your faith. That's success.

Truth 2: Your success is about your faithfulness, not your performance.

Sure, evaluate your knowledge and skills to see what you would like to add to your skill set, but also recognize that the Lord through His Spirit is the one who accomplishes conviction and conversion of the heart. Since we cannot talk someone into faith, our performance cannot be the measuring stick of success. Our job is to be faithful.

Truth 3: Your success is measured by your love, not the person's response.

When people don't respond like we hope, we can know that the apostles and the Lord Himself experienced rejection of their message in far more painful ways than we will ever experience. So, we remind ourselves that we share because of our love for the Lord and for the people who need the opportunity to accept or reject His offer of salvation, remembering that by God's grace the same opportunity was once offered to us.

Review–Success is . . .

Simply taking the opportunity to engage in spiritual conversations when we can and learning the skills to have better spiritual conversations more often!

THE "KNOW, SHARE, GROW" CYCLE

At Engage 360, the process of growing in ability to have spiritual conversations in everyday life involves a three-part cycle which we break down into: Know, Share, and Grow.

Master the Basics

We have a friend who is a former Army Ranger. He often tells people that what makes the Rangers elite is not their advanced tactics or gear. Rather, what makes this Special Ops Force the Army's premier light infantry unit is that they have absolute mastery over the basic skills. We take that same approach here. As we have seen, we have lots of fears that can keep us from sharing about Christ. We may lack knowledge or confidence, or we may fear how the listener might respond. Mastering the basics can help us deal with each of these concerns and enable us to turn conversations toward spiritual issues. But how do we master the basics?

KNOW

In order to share our faith, we have to have something to say.

We start out by mastering the basics of the Gospel message, learning what elements are essential to communicating the message efficiently and effectively.

SHARE

Once we have something to say, we can go say it. In this part, we follow through on our commitment to be intentional about looking for the opportunities God gives us and acting once we see them.

GROW

Once we get into a spiritual conversation, the conversation can go in many different directions. We might be asked a question we have never heard before, encounter a religion that is new to us, or interact with someone who doesn't understand even the basic aspects of Christianity. Almost every conversation will give us an opportunity to grow.

When we recognize we need to pursue learning something new in order to be able to meet the need of the non-Christian, we return to "Know" and the cycle continues.

CHALLENGE Ask someone you know who is a Christian why they are a Christian. Discuss with them the answer you gave at the beginning of this lesson. Remember to start where you are. If you aren't quite ready to take on the weekly challenge, give the Baby Step Challenge a try!

Baby Step Challenge

If talking to someone about their faith is too much for you right now, practice just saying "Hello" or "How are you?" to people you don't know.

You might be surprised how breaking the ice will open the door and give you confidence for the next challenge.

Prayer

Lord, I thank You for the opportunity to grow and to learn new skills that will enable me to engage in conversations that make a difference in someone's life here on earth and for eternity. Keep my mind clear and my heart focused on You and Your purposes, trusting You to guide and equip me by Your Spirit. In the name of Jesus. Amen.

Now I Know!

Sharing My Faith: Can I Do This?

. . .

I will start where I am. I will be honest about my fears and concerns. I will share them with the Lord and others on the same journey, trusting the Lord is working in me.

- I have examined my motives for sharing the Gospel. I ask forgiveness for unhealthy motives and choose to cultivate the following healthy motives for sharing the Gospel: a grateful heart for what Christ has done; a sincere burden for the lost; a loving obedience to Christ.
- I choose to measure success by: my own personal growth, not how well I compare with others; my faithfulness in sharing, not my performance; my love for people, not by their responses.
- In order to master the basics, I will learn and practice the truths of the Know, Share, Grow cycle in my life, will pray for opportunities to share my faith, and will be a support to fellow session members.

. . .

Find additional Session 1 resources at www.E360m.org/eywresources

Session 2
What Is The Gospel?

How then will they call on Him in whom they have not believed? And how are they to believe in Him of whom they have never heard? And how are they to hear without someone preaching? And how are they to preach unless they are sent? As it is written, "How beautiful are the feet of those who preach the good news!"

–Romans 10:14-15

...

We often assume that non-Christians understand what we mean by the word "Gospel," but many don't. Even as Christians we may need to clarify for ourselves what the word means and what are the essential basics of the Gospel message. We are going to do that in this chapter.

...

Read the exchange between Dyna Mo and A.G. Nostic, our non-Christian. Imagine if this were you talking to a friend.

(In as few words as possible, explain the Gospel to your friend.)

The Basics Of The Gospel Message

For a clear and concise definition of the Gospel, let's consider 1 Corinthians 15:3-8. Here Paul explains the Gospel (which literally means "good news"). Paul is explicit that he is reminding them of the Gospel that he preached to them. Paul "delivers" that which he "received." The use of these terms likely means Paul is using a process which would have been familiar to the Jews, as it is the same formula Jewish rabbis used to "pass on" teaching which they "received" from their rabbi.

After Paul's introductory comments in the first two verses of chapter 15, he presents what many scholars believe is the earliest Christian creed, likely dated to within a few years of the resurrection. Paul passes on this creed exactly as he received it.

Read 1 Corinthians 15:3-8 and underline or circle the following truth assertions:

1. Christ died for our sins in accordance with the Scriptures (Psalm 22)
2. He was buried (Isaiah 53:9)
3. He was raised on the third day in accordance with the Scriptures (Isaiah 53:10, Psalm 16:10)
4. He appeared to many people at different times (Luke 24:13-32, John 20:19-29, John 21, Acts 1:3-11)

While we often think of the Gospel as personal and relational, and rightly so, when we examine the 1 Corinthians 15:3-8 passage, we find that the verses are loaded with factual truth claims, evidence that can be verified. Look at the basic claims of the Gospel listed in the chart below.

The Gospel Basics

(1 Cor. 15:3-8)

Four Gospel Points	Why They Are Important
1. Jesus DIED	To cleanse us from sin
2. Jesus was BURIED	Demonstrates that He died
3. Jesus ROSE from the dead	Showed that He was the Son of God who successfully defeated death
4. Jesus APPEARED bodily to many people	Demonstrates that He rose from the dead

(2 PROVES 1; 4 PROVES 3)

...

Notice that points 1 and 3 are essential Gospel truths that are grounded in prophecies of the Old Testament Scriptures that foretold the events that would later happen to Christ: His death and resurrection.

Notice that points 2 and 4 are the supporting historical evidences that prove the events of 1 and 3 actually happened.

...

Using the information in the chart on the previous page, answer the following questions regarding the truth claims about Christ's death and resurrection.

What is the significance of the truth claim that Jesus was buried?	What does the fact of Jesus's bodily appearances to many people after his resurrection demonstrate?	What evidences are provided in these verses that confirm the Christian truth claims that Jesus died and rose to life again?

(Read Isaiah 53:8-10. This prophecy about the LORD's Servant (Messiah) was written about 700 years before Jesus lived.)

...

"The Scriptures"

The "Scriptures" to which Paul refers in our key passage are the sacred texts of the Old Testament, the Jews called the TaNaKh.

This was the Bible of Jesus and the disciples. These Old Testament Scriptures contain many prophecies about Messiah. Our Old Testament contains the same books as the Jewish TaNaKh but are numbered differently.

...

Compare each of the following Old Testament and New Testament verses, writing down the fact(s) about Jesus's death described by both.

Psalm 22:1
Matthew 27:46

Psalm 22:8
Matthew 27:43

Psalm 22:16-18
Matthew 27:35

HOW DO THESE OLD TESTAMENT PASSAGES SUPPORT THE CLAIMS OF THE GOSPEL ACCOUNTS OF JESUS'S DEATH IN THE NEW TESTAMENT?

The Apostle Peter tells us in 2 Peter 1:16, "For we [the apostles] did not follow cleverly devised myths when we made known to you the power and coming of our Lord Jesus Christ, but we were eyewitnesses of His majesty." This is truly good news! Some non-Christians reject Christianity because of bad experiences with Christians that make them think the Gospel is not true. Others reject the Gospel because they prefer that God does not exist. Still others reject the Gospel because they argue that it is narrow-minded, claiming to be the only way to God. Regardless of the reasons that non-Christians cite for rejecting the Gospel, the factual claims of the Gospel cannot be ignored. The Gospel claims that the historical event of Jesus's death and resurrection occurred and also provides supporting evidence for this claim. The transforming result of this claim is that if we turn from our sins to trust in what Jesus Christ did for us, our sins will be forgiven and we will be restored to a right relationship with God.

...

The Bodily Resurrection
Why is it important?
You will notice that when we talk about the resurrection we often say "bodily arose" or "physically arose."

This is important because some religions argue that Jesus arose "spiritually," not bodily. If this were the case, we would not be able to provide evidence for the resurrection.

The fact that Jesus arose bodily is a critical distinction and one that is confirmed by Scripture. (see John 20:28)

...

The Gospel Message In Contemporary Language

Jesus Christ died for our sins as was predicted in what we call the Old Testament. He was then buried in a tomb which proves that He was actually dead. On the third day He rose from the grave, as was predicted in the Old Testament, proving His victory over both sin and death. We know He was actually raised because He was seen by hundreds of people at different times and places. This is how we know Christianity is true and that Jesus can restore our broken relationship with God.

- Draw two lines under the two essential truths of the Gospel message.
- Draw a single line under the two supporting evidences of the essential truths.
- Check your answers by consulting the "Know the Gospel Basics" chart on page 28.

The Gospel Conversation

...

You might be thinking, "That sounds great, but I don't think it would make sense to walk up to someone and just start talking about the crucifixion and resurrection." We completely agree. Knowing the basics of the Gospel message is only one part of the Gospel conversation.

We also want to get to know the person by asking questions to learn what they think about God, Christianity, the Bible, church, etc., before presenting the Gospel message. (We will cover how to ask questions and present the Gospel in Sessions 4 and 5.).

Also, you may have heard it said that, "A person can't understand the good news until they understand the bad news about their sin and separation from God." We agree there needs to be a clear understanding of the problem that the Gospel solves. We also need to call for a response. We will dig into how to initiate and develop spiritual conversations in Sessions 4 and 5. For now, let's look at the big picture of the Gospel conversation.

...

It is helpful to think of our Gospel conversation as containing four main points:

1. Context of the Gospel

34 What is the problem the Gospel solves? Why do we need the Gospel in the first place?

2. Content of the Gospel

This is the solution, the four Gospel basics that Paul covers in 1 Corinthians 15:3-8.

3. Response to the Gospel

This is what a hearer of the Gospel message does in response to the gift of salvation God offers in the Gospel.

4. Results of the Gospel

This is what is gained by the person who accepts the Gospel by faith. Their broken relationship with God is restored, they receive the Holy Spirit, and they become a part of the Body of Christ (the Church).

(Fill in the blanks, using the information provided above, or try to fill in the blanks from memory.)

Context: What is the ______________ the Gospel solves?

Content: What is the ________________?

Response: This is what the hearer does when offered the ___________________ of salvation.

Results: This is what is ________________ by the person who accepts the Gospel by faith.

Pitfalls We Can Avoid

When sharing the Gospel, it is not just the content that is important. The way in which we present the content is crucial to ensure our message is understood by our listener. We can also use theological terms that non-Christians (as well as some Christians) do not understand. Avoiding these common pitfalls helps us share the Gospel clearly and escape derailing our evangelistic efforts.

There are three things we can do to overcome common pitfalls: delete unnecessary details, cut confusing "Christianese," and talk about more than your testimony.

1. Delete Distracting Details

...

A marketing company owner has described ideas as bowling balls. If you give someone one bowling ball, they should have no problem holding it. If you give them two bowling balls, they probably can hold them with some struggle. If you give them three bowling balls, they are likely to drop some or all of them.

Now imagine giving someone six bowling balls over the course of a 15-minute conversation. How many people will be successful in that scenario? How we communicate the Gospel can be a bit like the bowling ball example. As we share, we can add so many details that the person can become distracted by the irrelevant details and miss the main points.

...

Consider the following example of an attempt to share the Gospel.

I understand the challenge of your situation, and can see you are looking for hope in something more than your own strength. That is good, because you are a sinner from a long line of sinners going back all the way to Adam and Eve.

You see, God created the world in seven days, and Adam and Eve lived in the garden with all kinds of animals and trees, including the tree of the knowledge of good and evil, which God said they may not eat from. Eve was tempted to eat the fruit from that tree because she was deceived by a snake that was actually Satan.

So, you are a sinner like them, but God made a way for sin to be forgiven when Jesus was born from a virgin named Mary. Jesus lived a perfect life and performed many miracles, but made the religious leaders very mad.

They ended up crucifying Jesus between two thieves. After He died, He was buried in a tomb owned by Joseph of Arimathea, who was a member of the Sanhedrin, which was a ruling religious council that mostly hated Jesus.

When some of Jesus's female followers went to the tomb on the third day, the stone was rolled away, and they saw an angel who told them Jesus was gone. He had been raised from the dead victorious over sin and death, and then He ascended into heaven. Because of His death your sins can be forgiven, and Jesus's perfect life can become yours. Your hope is not in this world, but the reward of being in heaven with God and everyone who is saved. So, all you have to do is believe these things and accept the gift of salvation that God offers you in Jesus. Do you believe?

(In the presentation above, underline distracting details that are unnecessary to the essential Gospel message.)

...

While the preceding story is exaggerated for emphasis, we have heard well-meaning Christians include most of those details in actual evangelistic conversations or practice role plays.

You will have the chance to practice in your small group this week, and while it can be a bit awkward, role playing is an ideal way to practice in a safe environment where it is okay to make mistakes. It is a great opportunity to see what comes out when you start talking. Your partner can help you recognize unnecessary details you might want to remove from your presentation.

...

KEEP THIS SAYING IN MIND WHEN IT COMES TO ANY SPIRITUAL CONVERSATION, INCLUDING A GOSPEL CONVERSATION.

"EVERYTHING YOU SAY MUST BE TRUE, BUT YOU DON'T NEED TO SAY EVERYTHING THAT IS TRUE!"

When we present the Gospel message, some people will reject it. Regardless, our goal is to point people to Jesus and help them understand the clear and concise Gospel message. We need to avoid causing someone to think they are rejecting the Gospel, when they are actually rejecting a specific position on the age of the earth, certain miraculous stories in the Bible, or their own bad experiences with Christians. We also believe it is better for a person to knowingly reject the biblical Jesus and His Gospel than to accept a knockoff and think they have it figured out.

Our challenge is to grow in our ability to efficiently and effectively convey the Gospel message and the hope it provides. Once someone has accepted Jesus as the authority over sin and death and has accepted the gift of salvation offered through His death and resurrection, the discipleship process begins in earnest. There will be plenty of time to get into many important, interesting, and challenging theological discussions. But first they need to trust Jesus, not know how many animals fit on the ark.

The longer we are Christians the more likely we are to use language of the Christian culture that is unfamiliar to the rest of the world.

2. Cut Confusing "Christianese"

(Consider the following examples:)

- "You're a sinner in need of salvation, which can only be accomplished by the propitiatory sacrifice of Jesus for your atonement."
- "You need to repent for the forgiveness of your sins."
- "You need to be indwelled by the Holy Spirit."
- "You need to ask Jesus into your heart."

(Underline common Christian words/phrases in these sentences that may be unfamiliar or misunderstood by non-Christians. Discuss other words or phrases that could be confusing to a non-Christian, and can even be confusing for believers!)

3. Talk About More Than Your Testimony

...

For many years, we as Christians have been trained to share condensed versions of our testimonies of God's work in our life. The idea is to then offer the person with whom we are sharing the opportunity to receive the same benefits that we received in Christ. Here are some of the dangers with this approach:

...

- We can unintentionally glorify ourselves while minimizing Christ, in essence sending the message that we are the path to Jesus and they have to believe us first to get to Him. Instead, we should be pointing people to Jesus, whether they believe our testimony or not.
- Our experience may not be their experience. They may have different backgrounds, trials, challenges, etc., and God may work differently in their lives.
- Our testimonies often focus on the good benefits that we received when we trusted Christ as Savior, such as recovering from drug addiction, experiencing healing of a broken marriage, success at work, or an improved self-esteem. However, another person's story may not include these same benefits.
- We can share our testimonies without ever sharing the Gospel message.

While these are legitimate concerns, they do not need to keep us from sharing our testimony in a helpful way. Our testimony can be impactful and help create a bridge to the Gospel. This is especially the case when our testimony connects with the non-Christian in a personal way that enables us to understand things from their point of view or to find common ground.

At the same time, we want to point people to Christ and His power, focusing specifically on the results of the Gospel that the Scriptures affirm, as already discussed. In reality life might actually get a lot harder if they accept the Gospel, but the power of the Gospel is that we can have joy even in the midst of trials (See James 1:2, Romans 5:3-5, 1 Peter 1:6)

Describe the kind of person your testimony would be most likely to impact, keeping in mind that our testimony is only the connecting point and then the Gospel message points them to Christ.

____

____

CHALLENGE Ask someone you know, Christian or non-Christian, to share some commonly used Christian phrases or terms that they or others they know have found confusing. Brainstorm other words that can be used that are easier to understand.

Baby Step Challenge

If asking someone about commonly used terms that Christians use is a bit stressful for you, try asking a family member or friend about their experience with unfamiliar Christian phrases.

Prayer

Lord, I confess that I need Your enabling and guidance to share the Gospel effectively and in a way that honors You. Thank You for the truths You've shared with me in this session. Thank You for Your Holy Spirit who walks with me into every conversation and is working in the heart of non-Christians. Now, show me how and when to use what I've learned. Help me recall the context, content, response, and the results of the transforming Gospel message. Amen.

Now I Know!
What Is The Gospel?

The larger Gospel conversation includes the context, content, response, and results of the Gospel.

- The context of the Gospel is the problem of sin that the Gospel solves.
- The content of the Gospel includes the historical truths in 1 Corinthians 15:3-7 that Jesus died, was buried, bodily arose from the dead, and appeared to many people after His resurrection.
- The response to the Gospel consists of inviting the non-Christian to respond to Jesus by trusting Him as Savior.
- The results of the Gospel includes a restored relationship with God, the Holy Spirit entering the new believer's life, and becoming part of the family of God, called "the body of Christ."

The New Testament historical truth claims about Jesus's death and resurrection were prophesied in the Old Testament hundreds of years before the events occurred. This is strong evidence that the events of Jesus's death and resurrection actually occurred.

I can share the Gospel more effectively by:

- Deleting distracting details.
- Cutting confusing "Christianese."
- Talking about more than my testimony.

Find additional Session 2 resources at www.E360m.org/eywresources

Session 3
What the Gospel is Not

But if we or an angel from heaven should preach to you a Gospel contrary to the one we preached to you, let him be accursed.

–Galatians 1:8

...

The word Gospel literally means "good news," but people hold conflicting views on what that "good" message entails, often leading to aberrant teachings. We focused in the last chapter on the question, "What is the Gospel?" We now want to think about what the Gospel is not and learn how we can practice spiritual discernment that enables us to identify the true Gospel versus false or confused gospels by seeking to line up claims about the nature of the Gospel with what the Scripture actually says.

We will first look at biblical principles of discernment that will equip us to recognize the fake from the real. Then we will look at six of the most common misrepresentations of the Gospel.

...

Biblical Tools for Spotting False Gospels

Tool 1: Know The Scriptures

Tool 2: Spiritual Warfare

Tool 3: Watch For Lies Disguised As Truth

Tool 1: Know The Scriptures

Knowing the Gospel Basics, like we learned in Session 2, is the first tool to use in identifying false gospels. Let's do a quick review of the Gospel Basics.

(Fill in the blanks below and if you need a hint look back on pages 28 & 34. 1 Corinthians 15:3-8 might help as well.)

- Context: This is the ____________ the Gospel solves. It is called ____________.
- Content: Jesus ____________. Jesus was ____________. Jesus ____________ from the dead. Jesus ____________ to many people.
- Response: We ____________ what Christ did on the cross to pay for our sins ____________.
- Results: We are now in a right ____________ with God. We receive the Holy Spirit.

Tool 2: Spiritual Warfare

The Spiritual Battle over Truth

(Briefly describe what comes to mind when you think of "spiritual warfare.")

____

____

____

____

____

____

____

...

People answer this question in diverse ways. The idea of spiritual warfare often evokes fear, at least partially, because the concept has been misrepresented. So, we want to look at what the Bible has to say about spiritual warfare, so we can think about it in a way that equips us to recognize and respond to false presentations of the Gospel message.

...

Read 2 Corinthians 10:3-6
This passage explains the nature of our spiritual battle with false teachings. Notice that this passage affirms that spiritual warfare is primarily a battle of ideas.

Also notice that in this battle, one of the enemy's primary weapons is deception. Deception is rarely obvious, because it is wrapped in enough truth that many people, even Christians, miss it. But the deception tucked inside can lead to a false gospel or confusion that restricts the Gospel from spreading.

Below, write the two words in the passage that reveal that spiritual warfare is primarily a battle of ideas:

We destroy ______________________________

And every lofty ______________________________

Tool 3: Watch For Lies Disguised As Truth

Recognizing False Gospels
Read 2 Corinthians 11:13-15

FILL IN THE FOLLOWING BLANKS WITH THE CORRECT WORDS FROM THE SCRIPTURE PASSAGE!

. . .

We often think that false gospels arise only from secular culture, other religions, or views such as atheism.

While much deception arises from these sources, we contend that some of the most dangerous ideas are found within groups that self-identify as Christian or even from genuine Christians who are confused and unintentionally mislead people.

. . .

- False apostles appear as apostles of ________________________
- They copy their master, Satan, who disguises himself as an angel of ______________
- Satan's servants disguise themselves as servants of ______________

We've all heard of a wolf in sheep's clothing, but how many of us approach truth claims by self-identifying Christian speakers, teachers, and writers with the mindset that there is deception all around us? The answer is not to ignore all Christian teaching. Instead we suggest approaching the things you read and hear with the awareness that there are both well-meaning and not-so-well-meaning people who claim to speak truth, but instead lead people into embracing a false gospel.

LIST BELOW FALSE IDEAS OR CLAIMS YOU'VE HEARD ABOUT THE GOSPEL THAT UNDERMINE OR REPLACE THE TRUE GOSPEL.

____

____

____

____

...

Now, let's talk about six specific views that misrepresent the Gospel message.

The list is not exhaustive but highlights some of the most prevalent errors represented in our culture.

...

False Gospel 1: Works-Based Gospel

There is a delicate balance in the Christian life between the roles of grace and works. We can err in two directions regarding the role of works in salvation and the Christian life.

We can make works the basis on which we are saved on one extreme or we can make works irrelevant to faithful Christian practice on the other extreme.

Those who argue that we must do certain things or keep certain rules in order to be acceptable to God practice legalism.

Legalism is found in many legitimate Christian denominations, as well as in most cult movements. Legalism is not always blatant; it can be a subtle deviation that implies that Christianity is about being a good person and that being good makes us acceptable to God rather than trusting in the righteousness of Christ as the only way to acceptance by God.

Two Incorrect Extremes

Legalism: The idea that we must perform a certain act or work in order to gain or maintain our salvation.

Hyper-Grace: We have been saved by grace so our actions, thoughts, and deeds are now irrelevant.

Read the list of beliefs often held by people who think that salvation is a result of works. Below our points list any other beliefs that come to mind that show a works-based understanding of salvation. Don't forget to consider Christian PēCē's belief.

- "I can make up for my wrong deeds by doing good deeds."
- "If my good deeds outweigh my bad, I will go to heaven."
- "I will go to heaven as long as I confess my sins to a priest and do the penance he tells me to do."
- "I must believe in Jesus and live a good moral life to go to heaven."
- "I was baptized so I know I am saved."

____

____

____

____

____

Finding the balance of grace and works is one of the most common challenges to wrestle through in the Christian life.

It is true that our works do not earn our salvation or make us acceptable to God (Ephesians 2:8-9). We can never earn the forgiveness of our sins since only Christ as the perfect sacrifice could offer acceptable payment for our sins.

So, our good works as Christians are not the cause of our salvation, but the thankful result of our salvation and part of the process of being made more and more like Christ.

This truth stands in opposition not only to the claim that good works are required for salvation but also against the opposing view that because we are saved by grace and not works we can sin as much as we want, because with more sin comes more grace. This position may be called **"hyper grace"** today but in church history it has been called "antinomianism."

This view makes a mockery of Christ's sacrificial death and is sternly rebuked by Paul in his letter to the Romans: "What shall we say then? Are we to continue in sin that grace may abound? By no means!" (Romans 6:1).

Taking the idea of grace even further, another view, Universalism, holds that we are all going to heaven in the end. Regardless of our beliefs, God wouldn't send anyone to hell; it would be immoral for God to do so. A major challenge for Universalists is that Jesus frequently talks of the judgment and a separation that will occur.

For example, Jesus presents a separation of two similar but different things (Matthew 25:31-46, 3:12, 13:24-30, 13:3-9, Luke 16:19-31) such as: the sheep and the goats, the wheat and the chaff, the wheat and the tares, the fate of seeds scattered in different soil by the sower, or the parable of the rich man and Lazarus. While there are attempts made to use parts of the Bible to justify Universalism, a full analysis of these passages shows the Bible does not and cannot affirm Universalism.

The Bible clearly affirms God's love for all (including the lost who are separated at judgment) and on that point we can agree with the Universalists. Though it may be hard to understand this balance of God's love and His judgment, we can trust what Scripture teaches and develop a heart for the lost that gives us a passion and conviction to share the saving message of the Gospel.

False Gospel 2: Moralistic Therapeutic Deism

Another false portrayal of the Gospel is the idea that God exists to make me a better person and to fix my problems when I need Him.

Known as "Moralistic Therapeutic Deism (MTD)" this view is rampant in our culture. God can help me be a nicer person and do better things, but He really doesn't have any input in my daily life.

Central to this view is me, my self-esteem, my needs, and making myself a better person as I understand it.

(Read 1 Peter 2:24 and complete the following sentences)

- Problem according to MTD: I need to be a better person.
- Problem according to the Gospel: ________________
- Central figure in MTD: Me
- Central figure in the Gospel: ________________
- Goal in MTD: feel better about myself and be a better person.
- Goal in the Gospel: die to sin and ________________

...

The Gospel isn't about being a good person, reading your Bible, or opening the door for the elderly to earn God's favor. It's completely different! Check out this article to learn more about Moralistic Therapeutic Deism (MTD).

...

https://www.thegospelcoalition.org/article/mtd-not-just-a-problem-with-youth-ministry/

...

The Prosperity Gospel
The 'Good News' of the Gospel
is that God makes me healthy,
wealthy, and happy.

...

False Gospel 3: Prosperity Gospel

Called the "Prosperity Gospel," people who follow this view are known for their slogan, "name it and claim it," referring to the idea that if we have enough faith, God will give us health, wealth and blessings.

The sad truth is that many people who get drawn in to this deception become discouraged and abandon their faith when the disease they've earnestly prayed for doesn't get healed, the job doesn't come through, or the marriage they tried so hard to save, falls apart. They are told by their spiritual leaders of the Prosperity Gospel that they didn't receive a "yes" to their prayer because they didn't have enough faith. So, they try to conjure up more faith, to no end.

One of the greatest errors of this false gospel is the fact that it ignores the weight of the biblical evidence regarding suffering. If the Bible teaches us anything about the Christian life, it is that we will suffer. We suffer because we live in a fallen world. We suffer because of our own sin. We suffer because we are sinned against. A Gospel that ignores suffering as integral to the Christian life has deception written all over it.

Read John 16:33 and Romans 5:3-5 about suffering, then read the list below and identify each claim as a teaching of "PG" (Prosperity Gospel) or "CG" (Christ's Gospel).

______ Suffering happens because we don't have enough faith.

______ God promises to give us wealth in this world as Christians.

______ God promises to conform our character to Christ through suffering.

______ God does not want us to endure suffering here on earth.

______ If we believe God enough, we will have material blessings.

______ Suffering should be viewed as a temporary condition of this world.

...

Experience-based Gospel

The Gospel means you walk the aisle and get prayed over to get saved.

...

False Gospel 4: Experienced-based Gospel

An event can signify the point that we accept the Gospel and are brought into a right relationship with God through the forgiveness of our sin by trusting Christ. It is not wrong to associate the moment of salvation with a specific event, but it can be dangerous if we trust an event or an experience as the main evidence of our salvation.

Imagine you have an opportunity to share the Gospel with someone. After sharing, you ask the person if they have ever trusted Christ to be made right with God. Read the exchange between Christian PeCe and Dyna Mo to see what that conversation might look like.

WELL, I ACCEPTED JESUS AS MY SAVIOR.

HOW DID THAT HAPPEN FOR YOU?

WHEN I WAS SIX AT MY GRANDMA'S CHURCH THE PREACHER TOLD US TO COME UP FRONT IF WE WANTED TO GET SAVED, SO I WENT UP FRONT.

SO WHAT DOES IT MEAN TO YOU TO BE SAVED?

WELL, YOU GET BAPTIZED AND JOIN THE CHURCH, YOU KNOW. AND GOD HELPS YOU LIVE A GOOD MORAL LIFE AND THEN YOU GO TO HEAVEN.

AND IF THAT IS WHAT IT MEANS, HOW DO YOU GET SAVED?

WELL, LIKE I SAID, IT'S WALKING UP FRONT AND HAVING THE PREACHER PRAY OVER YOU.

At this point, you know there are several gaps in the person's understanding of the Gospel content and the response that leads to salvation. The problem may be that they are not able to verbally express what salvation involves. But it could also be true that they are not saved. Either way, we have a great opportunity to help disciple them along!

With this example, it's easy to see the danger of thinking that an event or experience means salvation regardless of belief or understanding of what it means to be saved. Be aware that each person may include different significant points in their salvation experience. Perhaps they think that they joined the church or were baptized to be saved.

List some of the Gospel basics that are missing from Christian PēCē's testimony on p. 58. You may want to use biblical tool 1 to help your friend come to a better understanding of the Gospel.

____

____

____

____

____

. . .

"'Social justice' is not the Gospel. It was not Jesus' message. It was not why He came. His real message was much more radical. Jesus' teaching—and the Story itself—focuses on something else. Not on the works of Christians, but rather on the work of Christ. That is what the Story teaches."
*Gregory Koukl, Christian apologist, "The Rescue: Why Did Jesus Come,"
–Stand to Reason
https://www.str.org/w/the-rescue-why-did-jesus-come-

. . .

False Gospel 5: Social Justice Gospel

A major topic in our world today is "social justice." Social justice has taken multiple forms and is invoked on a variety of different issues. The challenge for the Christian with regard to social justice is a question of balance and priority.

Social justice is another area that can be a direct and intentional Gospel replacement, where Christianity is remade to focus on bringing societal improvement in the world. Of course, bringing improvement to the world and individual lives can be very good. However, that is not the Gospel message of 1 Corinthians 15, nor the rest of the New Testament.

Perhaps the bigger threat is not from those who replace the biblical Gospel with social justice, but from the shift in focus from the Gospel to ones social justice effort. The Gospel is not rejected, just minimized or hidden away.

Similar to works-based teaching about the Gospel, social justice presents the Gospel as a broader, more panoramic remedy for the ills and injustices of our culture.

It is true that as Christians we are called to seek justice, care for those in need, and stand for righteousness, including helping our neighbors, caring for those in need (James 1:27), fighting for the lives of the unborn, and opposing racism. If we are not standing for righteousness within our communities and in our nation, we are not following the steps of our Lord.

At the same time, we must also make clear that these acts of righteousness are not the essence of the Gospel message. Remember that we asserted that good works are the result, rather than the cause, of our salvation.

The fact that Christians impact their culture through righteous acts is also a result, rather than a cause, of salvation. Service in the interest of justice does not change the corrupt human heart; the redeemed human heart is changed by Christ so that we do acts of service with an eternal purpose.

Any "religious" act of service that attempts to replace the core message of the death of Christ for the forgiveness of sin and the resurrection as proof of His victory over death and sin is a false gospel.

There have been many projects and mission trips that had the best of intentions to serve the needs of a group and then share with them about Christ and the Gospel. The problem is that often the focus has been put into planning and implementing the service projects with little to no planning on how to share about Christ in a meaningful and effective way.

The end result is a whole lot of service with very little Gospel. Remember Jesus's own teaching in Matthew 16:26, "For what will it profit a man if he gains the whole world and forfeits his soul? Or what shall a man give in return for his soul?" We could eliminate starvation from the face of the earth (and should try to do so) but if we do not deal with the spiritual starvation of the world then we have failed.

That being said, we also cannot pretend to serve and care merely to get an opportunity to share a few Bible verses with those we serve. Our service should be genuine and borne out of a heart for those made in God's image.

That heart should also drive us to learn enough about the people we serve to effectively share the ultimate hope found in the Gospel, to bring spiritual healing and restored relationship with God leading to an eternal reward that cannot perish!

As we think of the need to stand for righteousness in our culture, let's also affirm that the source of our righteousness is not the act itself, but the Lord Jesus Who enables us to die to sin and live for righteousness through His sacrificial death on the cross.

(List several actions that you or other Christians you know have taken to stand for righteousness in our culture.)

. . .

Gnostic/Mystic Gospel

What is most important is to attain a higher spiritual status through secret knowledge or have special spiritual experiences.

. . .

False Gospel 6: Gnostic/Mystic Gospel

One of the most common false gospels has been around since the beginning of the Church and is known as Gnosticism. Gnosticism means "secret knowledge", and infers that the key to the Christian life, personal growth, or attaining salvation is based on attaining some secret knowledge. It may be that this knowledge gives us power over our sin, access to power to create success, financial increase, or happiness. Often there is a need for commitment to a specific leader or group who grants access to the knowledge, and often at a financial cost to achieve higher levels.

> "Gnosticism as a philosophy refers to a related body of teachings that stress the acquisition of 'gnosis', or inner knowledge. The knowledge sought is not strictly intellectual, but mystical; not merely a detached knowledge of or about something, but a knowing by acquaintance or participation. This gnosis is the inner and esoteric mystical knowledge of ultimate reality. It discloses the spark of divinity within, thought to be obscured by ignorance, convention, and mere esoteric religiosity."
>
> –Douglas Groothius
> 'Gnosticism and the Gnostic Jesus," Christian Research Journal, April 21, 2009
> https://www.equip.org/articles/gnosticism-and-the-gnostic-jesus/

Somewhat related to Gnosticism is Mysticism, which focuses on having special spiritual experiences. While it is possible to have a legitimate spiritual experience, the danger comes in focusing on the experience rather than the truth of the real-life events of the death, burial, and resurrection of Christ, and taking that message to a lost and dying world.

Also, any spiritual experience mediated by a "familiar spirit" or a "spiritual guide" is a sign of a false gospel and exposes the person to demonic influence. This influence does not require a physical takeover of the body but can be guiding to a bad idea or practice that inhibits the Gospel going forth. This is why seeking these experiences are forbidden by God.

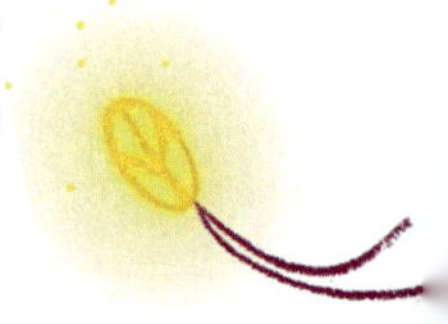

...

We should be aware that even for a Christian seeking to follow the Lord, an effective deceptive method of the enemy is to divert our attention from sharing the Gospel to focusing on our personal religious practice and experiences.
When this happens, we become useless to the greater Body of Christ in spreading the Gospel. We need to be careful to balance personal spiritual practices with corporate worship, acts of service, and sharing the Gospel message.

...

Read the list below. Identify each description as characteristic of GM (Gnosticism/Mysticism) or GC (Gospel of Christ):

_____ We should focus on inner special spiritual experiences.

_____ We are to focus on the reality of the death and resurrection of Jesus Christ.

_____ Humans naturally have a spark of divinity within them.

_____ Humans are created beings made in the image of God, but not divine themselves.

_____ Christ enters someone's life by repentance from sin and trusting Christ.

_____ We can become aware of the spark of divinity when we get rid of ignorance and religiosity.

CHALLENGE Engage a Christian in a conversation, asking them what it means to be a Christian, what it takes to go to heaven, or what it takes to be right with God. Identify whether their response reflects any of the six false gospels.

Baby Step Challenge

Start where you are. Find someone from your church and ask them what it takes to go to heaven and identify if their response reflects the true Gospel.

Prayer

Lord Jesus, may I remember that the true Gospel message consists only of Your death and resurrection. No other gospel provides true hope. Amen.

Now I Know!

What The Gospel Is Not

...

Biblical tools for discerning whether a particular religious view is teaching a true or false Gospel.

- Tool #1 – Know the Scriptures (Know the Gospel Basics). Examine the Context, Content, Response, and Result the religious view teaches to see if they align with the biblical teaching.
  Tool #2 – Spiritual Warfare
- Spiritual warfare is most accurately characterized as a battle of ideas, a confrontation between truth and deception.
- Tool #3 – Watch for Lies Disguised as Truth
  Satan's deception often goes unnoticed because it is embedded in truth.

Six False Gospels Include

Works-based Gospel	Experience-based Gospel
Moralistic Therapeutic Deism	Social Justice Gospel
Prosperity Gospel	Gnostic/Mystic Gospel

...

Find additional Session 3 resources at www.E360m.org/eywresources

Session 4

Sharing The Gospel Like An Apostle

For though I am free from all, I have made myself a servant to all, that I might win more of them. To the Jews I became as a Jew, in order to win Jews. To those under the law I became as one under the law (though not being myself under the law) that I might win those under the law. To those outside the law I became as one outside the law (not being outside the law of God but under the law of Christ) that I might win those outside the law. To the weak I became weak, that I might win the weak. I have become all things to all people, that by all means I might save some. I do it all for the sake of the gospel, that I may share with them in its blessings.

–I Corinthians 9:19-23

...

We have learned what the Gospel is and what it is not. Now, in the next two sessions we will learn how to share the Gospel message through conversations in everyday life and how to use biblical principles to do so.

You may know of certain evangelistic methods or structured presentations that are designed to help you share the Gospel. We believe many can be useful in the right situation and consider them like tools on a tool belt.

But have you ever considered the evangelistic methods used by the apostles, such as Peter and Paul, at the beginning of the Church? We often read Acts and the Epistles to learn about the early church and to gain principles for Christian life. However, we may not have realized that there are great examples of how to share the Gospel in different contexts giving us principles we can apply today. In this lesson we will look at two of those examples from very different contexts and learn about the tactics Paul and Peter used when sharing the Gospel.

...

A Helpful Acronym

The acronym **G.O.S.P.E.L.** will help us remember some biblical principles to guide spiritual conversations and help us to be more effective in sharing the Gospel.

We will see how both Peter and Paul include the same steps to sharing the Gospel message, represented by the acronym **"GOSPEL"**, while at the same time tailoring the message to the specific needs of each audience.

G — Gauge your audience
O — Offer common ground
S — Shift to the Gospel
P — Provide evidence
E — Explain the Gospel
L — Leave with a clear next step

Based on each brief description on the left, which of the steps do you think will be easiest for you? The hardest?

____

____

____

____

Now, let's take a look at two great biblical examples of how to share the Gospel message

- The Apostle Peter's sermon at Pentecost in Acts 2
- The Apostle Paul's speech at Mars Hill in Acts 17

Peter's Gospel-Sharing Approach with the Jews: Acts 2:14-41

Pentecost occurred on the fiftieth day after Passover. Jews from numerous nations had traveled to Jerusalem to participate in Passover. Peter preached to Jews on the first Pentecost celebration after Jesus's resurrection and ascension. Peter's sermon is important because the numerous faith responses to his message spawned the early church and spread the Gospel into diverse parts of the world.

The verses prior to the ones we are studying describe the Holy Spirit making His presence known as a "mighty rushing wind," appearing as "tongues as of fire" upon the disciples. They were enabled to share "the mighty works of God" and be heard in the native languages of the numerous Jewish visitors from other nations. Hearing the message in their individual languages, some were inquisitive, and others thought the hearers were drunk.

(Read the biblical account of Peter's sermon in Acts 2:14-41 in preparation for a detailed look at the passage.)

...

In Peter's sermon we see important information he communicates to his audience that becomes a pattern for what Peter includes in his Gospel messages.

The G.O.S.P.E.L. acronym will help remind us of the important information to include when sharing the truth of the Gospel.

...

Gauge your audience

In verse 14, who was Peter's audience?

____

The fact that Peter's audience consisted of Jews meant that they, like Peter, would be familiar with the Old Testament scriptures and the promised Messiah.

Acts 2:14

But Peter, standing with the eleven, lifted up his voice and addressed them: "Men of Judea and all who dwell in Jerusalem, let this be known to you, and give ear to my words."

Offer common ground

Given that his listeners were Jewish, as was Peter, how did he offer common ground between his listeners and himself?

____

____

Shift to the Gospel

How did Peter shift his presentation to the Gospel?

____

____

Acts 2:15-21

For these people are not drunk, as you suppose, since it is only the third hour of the day. But this is what was uttered through the prophet Joel: "And in the last days it shall be, God declares, that I will pour out my Spirit on all flesh, and your sons and your daughters shall prophesy, and your young men shall see visions, and your old men shall dream dreams; even on my male servants and female servants in those days I will pour out my Spirit, and they shall prophesy. And I will show wonders in the heavens above and signs on the earth below, blood, and fire, and vapor of smoke; the sun shall be turned to darkness and the moon to blood, before the day of the Lord comes, the great and magnificent day. And it shall come to pass that everyone who calls upon the name of the Lord shall be saved.'

Acts 2:22

"Men of Israel, hear these words: Jesus of Nazareth, a man attested to you by God with mighty works and wonders and signs that God did through him in your midst, as you yourselves know—..."

We want to remember that our goal is not simply to offer common ground with our listeners but to get to the Gospel message. Peter did not stop with the Old Testament prophet Joel's prophecy but shifted to the Gospel by turning his listeners' attention toward what they knew about the miraculous events surrounding Jesus Christ. Notice that Peter didn't start with the claim of Jesus's deity and resurrection but pointed out what they themselves had witnessed.

Provide evidence

Look at the list of evidences below that Dyna Mo is telling us about. Peter provided these evidences to his listeners to support his claim that Jesus was the long-awaited Messiah in whom they should trust. In the scripture passage on p. 75, underline any of the evidences you find.

JESUS'S FULFILLMENT OF OLD TESTAMENT PROPHECY BY DAVID IN WHICH DAVID FORESAW THAT GOD'S "HOLY ONE" WOULD NOT BE ABANDONED TO HADES OR SEE CORRUPTION IN DEATH

(POINTING TO THE FACT THAT HE WOULD ARISE FROM THE DEAD)

THE EVENT OF JESUS'S CRUCIFIXION OF WHICH THEY WERE ALL AWARE

JESUS'S RESURRECTION OF WHICH THE APOSTLES WERE EYEWITNESSES

Read Acts 2:23-31

"...this Jesus, delivered up according to the definite plan and foreknowledge of God, you crucified and killed by the hands of lawless men. God raised Him up, loosing the pangs of death, because it was not possible for Him to be held by it. For David says concerning Him, "'I saw the Lord always before me, for He is at my right hand that I may not be shaken; therefore my heart was glad, and my tongue rejoiced; my flesh also will dwell in hope. For you will not abandon my soul to Hades, or let your Holy One see corruption. You have made known to me the paths of life; you will make me full of gladness with your presence.' "Brothers, I may say to you with confidence about the patriarch David that he both died and was buried, and his tomb is with us to this day. Being therefore a prophet, and knowing that God had sworn with an oath to him that he would set one of his descendants on his throne, he foresaw and spoke about the resurrection of the Christ, that he was not abandoned to Hades, nor did his flesh see corruption..."'

...

In a spiritual conversation, as we gauge our audience and learn about them, we will find that varying levels of evidence are needed. There may be times that very little is required but it seems that every time an evangelistic message is given in the New Testament at a minimum the resurrection is mentioned as the essential proof of the Gospel.

In Peter's case, he knew his audience well enough to anticipate their questions without their verbalizing them. The Jews anticipated the coming of the Messiah. Their unspoken question was, How do we know this Jesus of Nazareth is the Messiah?

Our listeners may also have questions such as, Is there a God, and if so, which God is it? They may have questions about Christian practices and why they differ. They may wonder if the Bible can be trusted or if it has been changed to give certain groups or people power. An important step is to be aware of and open to people asking these kinds of questions. We can also prepare ourselves with answers to these questions. We will cover some of the most essential basics for being able to explain that the Gospel is true in lesson 6.

For now, know that providing evidence in response to questions enables us to keep the conversation open and moving forward. We should also be aware that questions may arise about Christianity before or after we share the Gospel. Knowing this will help us keep the conversation on track and directed toward Jesus Christ and His salvation.

...

Explain the Gospel message

In his message to the Jews, Peter quoted Psalm 110:1. Written by David, Psalm 110 says that the LORD (Yahweh) speaks to the Lord (Adonai), another name for the Messiah.

Messiah Adonai:
- Sits at Yahweh's right hand
- Is a priest forever
- Will execute judgment over all the nations

So, Peter's listeners were aware of these prophetic characteristics of the coming Messiah. Reading the passage from Acts 2, underline the phrases that repeat one of the three divine acts of Messiah from Psalm 110:1.

Read Acts 2:32-36

This Jesus God raised up, and of that we all are witnesses. Being therefore exalted at the right hand of God, and having received from the Father the promise of the Holy Spirit, He has poured out this that you yourselves are seeing and hearing. For David did not ascend into the heavens, but he himself says, "'The Lord said to my Lord, "Sit at my right hand, until I make your enemies your footstool." Let all the house of Israel therefore know for certain that God has made him both Lord and Christ, this Jesus whom you crucified."

Referring to Acts 2, select from one of the words Dyna Mo can't help but share to complete each blank in the summary below.

- Peter affirms that it is this Jesus whom God "________________ up."
- He was ________________ to the right hand of God, and poured out the Holy __________ on the people, which the people were now seeing and hearing.
- This Messiah Jesus would execute judgment, making His enemies His __________, showing His power and authority as God.
- This is the same Messiah whom they had killed by ________________ .

Consulting the summary on the previous page, fill in the blanks below with the two Gospel basics that must be presented when we share the Gospel message: (Hint: We learned about them in chapter two!)

Jesus's C ______________________________

Jesus's R ______________________________

Both Jesus's death and resurrection are essential basic elements of the Gospel message. Jesus's death is crucial because in order for the resurrection to be true, Jesus must first have physically died. In fact, some belief systems, such as Islam argue that Jesus did not really die on the cross. Other belief systems argue that He did not really rise from the dead. Recall that Jehovah's Witnesses argue that Jesus did not rise physically, only spiritually. So false religions often deny one or both of these two essential basics of the Gospel message. That is why we must make clear these basic claims of the Gospel. Without them, what we are sharing is not the genuine Gospel message.

Leave with a clear next step

Every time we have a spiritual conversation, we should leave the person we are talking to with a clear next step. This step may differ based on your relationship with the person, how often you see them, what you discussed in the conversation, and more.

In some conversations, this will mean asking the person if they are ready to accept the Gospel and forgiveness of their sins. In other conversations, it may mean asking them to read a book about how we can trust the Bible or know that God is real. The key is to give a clear next step. Following through on giving a clear next step may come more naturally for those who are gifted in evangelism or for those who are natural extroverts.

However, in our observations, one of the biggest reasons for the effectiveness of the conversations that evangelists have compared to other Christians, is that evangelists give the person they are speaking with a clear next step.

Our team may not always agree with (or condone) some of the methods used by some evangelists, but we agree that a clear next step allows people the opportunity to choose to respond, one way or the other. We will discuss the variety of action steps you can give in the next session.

Read Acts 2:37-41

Now when they heard this they were cut to the heart, and said to Peter and the rest of the apostles, "Brothers, what shall we do?" And Peter said to them, "Repent and be baptized every one of you in the name of Jesus Christ for the forgiveness of your sins, and you will receive the gift of the Holy Spirit. For the promise is for you and for your children and for all who are far off, everyone whom the Lord our God calls to Himself." And with many other words he bore witness and continued to exhort them, saying, "Save yourselves from this crooked generation." So those who received his word were baptized, and there were added that day about three thousand souls.

Explain briefly how the listeners responded to Peter's message.

____

____

____

____

As Christians, we often avoid this crucial final step because we fear that the listener may say "no," or we don't want to make people uncomfortable. But this is an important step for the non-Christian. Whether it is learning more about Christianity or accepting the offer of salvation found in the Gospel, a clear next step is a great way to keep the person from staying neutral or passive. They have to make an intentional decision to consider or to reject.

If the step is considering to trust in Jesus Christ, this clarifies that they cannot be neutral about the Gospel. Even when they say "no," they must deal with the implications of their rejection of the Gospel. We have no responsibility for making them move forward, but we do have the wonderful opportunity to give them a clear path.

How is the response of the listeners in the passage below different from how listeners often respond when we share the Gospel message?

____

____

____

____

Read Acts 2:42-47

And they devoted themselves to the apostles' teaching and the fellowship, to the breaking of bread and the prayers. And awe came upon every soul, and many wonders and signs were being done through the apostles. And all who believed were together and had all things in common. And they were selling their possessions and belongings and distributing the proceeds to all, as any had need. And day by day, attending the temple together and breaking bread in their homes, they received their food with glad and generous hearts, praising God and having favor with all the people. And the Lord added to their number day by day those who were being saved.

Peter told his listeners that they needed to respond by doing what two things?

____

UNDERLINE THE FAITH RESPONSES OF PETER'S LISTENERS IN ACTS 2:42-47

Recall that to be saved, someone must turn from trusting his own works to trusting Christ's sufficient and final work on the cross for salvation. Self-trust is sin.

That's what repentance means in the context of the Gospel: to agree with what God says about our sin condition and to turn away from one's sin to Christ.

You could summarize what you have underlined by saying that the manifestations of God's working among Christians in this early church included specific evidences of God's intervention, as well as specific acts and attitudes among the Christian community.

Let's review the acronym we are using to help us remember the six principles to spiritual conversations and sharing the Gospel.

See how many of the blanks below that you can fill in without looking back at the answers. Once finished, check your answers and make corrections, as needed.

G — Gauge ____________________

O — Offer ____________________

S — Shift ____________________

P — Provide ____________________

E — Explain ____________________

L — Leave ____________________

Compare what you've underlined in Acts 2:42-47 with the list below.

- Devotion to the apostles' teaching
- Fellowship
- Corporate prayer
- Togetherness-unity
- Generosity
- Attitude of praise toward God
- Evidences of God's working among them through wonders and signs
- A sense of awe at God's work among them
- Sharing of physical possessions, as needed
- Regular corporate worship
- Sharing meals together

Paul's Gospel-Sharing Approach with the Athenians: Acts 17:16-34

Now, let's apply the acronym 'GOSPEL' to our second example, in which the Apostle Paul shared the Gospel in an entirely different setting from that of Peter's. Fill in the blanks, stating the action for each letter of the acronym from memory as you go along. Make corrections, as needed.

G________________

Underline the phrases that illustrate Paul knew the following things about his audience:

- They were very religious and polytheistic and worshiped idols.
- They were fascinated with new ideas and new deities.
- They wanted to understand the world around them and how it worked

Recall that Paul was a devout and well-trained Jew. So, he knew the Hebrew Scriptures well. But this passage reveals that he also knew something about the Greek culture and their religious beliefs and practices.

Acts 17:16-21

Now while Paul was waiting for them at Athens, his spirit was provoked within him as he saw that the city was full of idols. So he reasoned in the synagogue with the Jews and the devout persons, and in the marketplace every day with those who happened to be there. Some of the Epicurean and Stoic philosophers also conversed with him. And some said, "What does this babbler wish to say?" Others said, "He seems to be a preacher of foreign divinities"—because he was preaching Jesus and the resurrection. And they took him and brought him to the Areopagus, saying, "May we know what this new teaching is that you are presenting? For you bring some strange things to our ears. We wish to know therefore what these things mean." Now all the Athenians and the foreigners who lived there would spend their time in nothing except telling or hearing something new.

. . .

Epicureanism is often thought of as an ancient philosophy that teaches self-indulgence and pleasure.

But it actually taught that it is best to order life in a way to live free from stress, even the stress caused by excessive pleasure-seeking.

Stoicism was pantheistic, arguing that the material world was all there was, and that people should align their expectations with the natural law of the cosmos called the logos (consider John 1:1).

. . .

https://www.gotquestions.org/Stoicism-Stoic.html, 7-3-20

O ______________________

Paul's listeners already recognize that he is very religious. So he takes the opportunity to affirm this conviction they hold in common. In acknowledging that he recognizes that they are very religious he offers common ground with his listeners, earning the right to be heard.

Acts 17:22-23

So Paul, standing in the midst of the Areopagus, said: "Men of Athens, I perceive that in every way you are very religious. For as I passed along and observed the objects of your worship, I found also an altar with this inscription: 'To the unknown god.'

What inscription does Paul notice on an altar that he uses as a springboard for discussion?

____

. . .

Epimenides, a revered Cretan philosopher and poet, had evidently saved the city from a plague hundreds of years prior to Paul's message by proclaiming the existence of an unknown god and by building altars of worship to him. Paul's knowledge of this cultural nuance is revealed in the fact that he referred in Titus 1:12-13 to a line from Epimenides's poetry. His cultural knowledge served him well in gaining a hearing, and we should follow his lead.

John Argubright, "To the Unknown God," Biblehistory.com, 2013

. . .

S________________

Look at what Paul does. He affirms that they worship an "unknown god." Then, he claims that this god about which they do not know (but have included to avoid forgetting one), he will explain to them. There indeed is an unknown God that they can know personally!

Acts 17:23b
What therefore you worship as unknown, this I proclaim to you.

Paul's shift to the Gospel includes information that the Jewish people, to whom Peter spoke, did not need to know. The Jewish people already knew about the one, true God Yahweh, and questioned whether this Jesus was the Messiah that God sent. But the pagan Greeks worshiped many false gods, and before they could know the Christ whom God sent, they first had to figure out who this God was!

P________________

Paul recognized that the pagan Greek listeners within his audience did not already know about the one, true God of the Jewish people. So, Paul provided evidence designed specifically to meet the needs of this pagan Greek audience who worshiped many different gods.

Before they could learn about the Christ Whom God sent, they first needed to understand that the one, true God was nothing like their capricious, superhuman, but fault-ridden pantheon of Greek gods.

Acts 17:24-29
The God who made the world and everything in it, being Lord of heaven and earth, does not live in temples made by man, nor is he served by human hands, as though he needed anything, since He himself gives to all mankind life and breath and everything. And He made from one man every nation of mankind to live on all the face of the earth, having determined allotted periods and the boundaries of their dwelling place, that they should seek God, and perhaps feel their way toward Him and find Him. Yet He is actually not far from each one of us, for "'In Him we live and move and have our being'; as even some of your own poets have said, "'For we are indeed His offspring.' Being then God's offspring, we ought not to think that the divine being is like gold or silver or stone, an image formed by the art and imagination of man.

How do you think the God that Paul described in the passage on the previous page differed from the ancient Greek gods?

___

___

The information that Paul shared about God provided the context for the Gospel he was about to share. This God loved humans and initiated a relationship with them. He also laid out the necessary requirements for a relationship with Him as a holy, infinite, Being. And this is where the Gospel comes in!

E_______________

Note that Paul combines both basic elements of the Gospel in a single phrase. Underline that phrase.

Recall that Peter called his listeners to repentance. Write below what it means to repent in order to be saved. (Look back at the section on Peter's message for help.)

Acts 17:30-31

...He commands all people everywhere to repent, because He has fixed a day on which He will judge the world in righteousness by a man whom He has appointed; and of this He has given assurance to all by raising him from the dead.

___

___

L________________

Remember that we always want to call the listener to respond to the Gospel message. In the previous passage, Acts 17:30-31, we not only see the basics of the Gospel message included, but also that Paul calls the listeners to do something.

Acts 17:32-34

Now when they heard of the resurrection of the dead, some mocked. But others said, "We will hear you again about this." 33 So Paul went out from their midst. 34 But some men joined him and believed, among whom also were Dionysius the Areopagite and a woman named Damaris and others with them.

What did he call them to do? ____________________

List peoples' different responses to Paul's message. ____________________

What do the varied responses of Paul's listeners tell us about how people may respond to us when we share the Gospel with them? ____________________

____

Comparing Acts 2 and Act 17

What did Peter and Paul do that was similar in sharing the Gospel?

____

____

____

What did they do that was different?

____

____

____

Why do you think they each took the approach that they did?

____

____

____

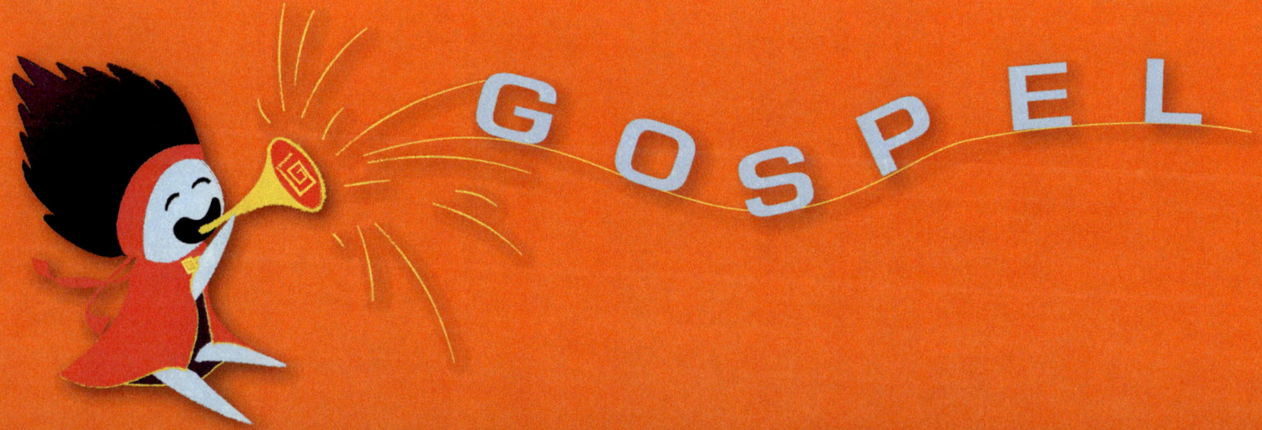

CHALLENGE

In the spirit of Paul when he was in Athens, do a spiritual analysis of your city and your neighborhood.

Drive around your town/city and make observations of anything that gives you insight into the spiritual state of the people living there. Note anything that sticks out to you in addition to these areas:

- What do you see that gives you an idea of what gives life meaning?
- What do you see that tells you what people highly value?
    - In what ways are people religious?
    - What topics are of interest for people to learn?

Baby Step Challenge

Adjust the challenge for what you can do. You may want to observe where people in your community gather.

Prayer

Lord, thank You for opening my eyes to the truth of who You are and what You have done for me. Please give me discernment and understanding to see the hindrances and obstacles that stand against the truth of the Gospel, and creative ways to communicate the message that brings light and life to all who believe. Amen.

Now I Know!

Share the Gospel Like an Apostle

- How the apostles shared the Gospel in Acts
- The similarities and differences Peter and Paul used to address very different audiences.
- That I need to consider how I can apply the principles Peter and Paul used in my own conversations

Gauge your audience:
Take time to ask questions

Offer common ground:
Present Christianity in a way that will resonate with them.

Shift to the Gospel:
Turn the conversation toward spiritual matters.

Provide evidence:
To show that God exists, then direct the conversation toward the Gospel.

Explain the Gospel:
Avoid Christianese and explain Christianity and the Gospel in a way that will make sense to the person with whom you are speaking.

Leave with a clear next step:
Leave the person we are speaking to with a clear next step to either accept the Gospel or move closer toward it.

Find additional Session 4 resources at www.E360m.org/eywresources

Session 5

How To Have Spiritual Conversations

For this very reason, make every effort to supplement your faith with virtue, and virtue with knowledge, and knowledge with self-control, and self-control with steadfastness, and steadfastness with godliness, and godliness with brotherly affection, and brotherly affection with love. For if these qualities are yours and are increasing, they keep you from being ineffective or unfruitful in the knowledge of our Lord Jesus Christ

–2 Peter 1:5-8

. . .

It's always good to learn new things, but knowledge finds its true value when it is applied. Everything we have covered in the last several weeks—all of the principles illustrated by the acronym G.O.S.P.E.L.— have been preparing us to put our knowledge into action so that we can help people move toward God.

In this lesson, we will learn seven keys to successfully starting and guiding spiritual conversations.

- TALK; don't preach.
- GUARD your conversation as a "No Christianese" zone.
- SHOW genuine interest.
- KNOW the person you are talking with.
- LOOK for opportunities to be on "their side."
- REMEMBER that Jesus is right, not us.
- ASK three questions when presented with a challenge.

Read out loud the seven keys above which outline successful engagement in spiritual conversations. Underline the action word(s) in each sentence.

. . .

Talk. Don't Preach

While the principles for sharing the Gospel, as discussed previously, could be used for street preaching or door-to-door evangelism, we want to focus on sharing your faith in everyday life within normal conversations with family, friends, neighbors or co-workers. Therefore, we want to focus on conversational approaches to speaking with people rather than preaching at them.

We have learned from experience that when someone thinks you are preaching at them rather than talking with them, they are more likely to shut down.

There may be times when a person you are talking with is open and receptive to the Gospel message. When this opportunity arises, we want to share with them in a conversational, and when possible, interactive style.

Briefly describe a situation in which you or someone else tried to share Christianity in a way that was more "preaching at" than "talking with" the person. What was the impact?

____

____

____

____

Guard Your Conversation As A "No-Christianese" Zone

If you were in North Carolina and asked someone a question, what language would you speak? Most likely, you would speak English. But have you ever thought about the fact that there are words that are common to some American English speakers that would sound like a foreign language to other American English speakers?

Consider a funny story from one of our team members who moved from Nebraska to North Carolina for seminary. The first time they went to the grocery store, someone greeted them and said, "Would you like a buggy?" Totally confused, the Nebraskan looked back at them with a blank stare. Now, if you grew up or spent time in the Southern United States, you might be laughing right now. If not, you may be confused like the Nebraskan, unaware that in North Carolina, a buggy is a shopping cart.

While shopping carts do not have eternal significance, the Gospel does! Given the eternal significance of spiritual conversations, we need to be sure we are not talking about buggies in a world that only knows about shopping carts.

As we begin to have more spiritual conversations, we can think about the words and phrases we use. Christian terms that may be clear and normal to us may be confusing to the non-Christian with whom we are talking.

We can guard our conversations so that they are free of confusing Christian terms. In this way, we are being thoughtful in what we say and also for what our listener is hearing.

Our team offers a one-day evangelism training for churches. In the training we play a video that often makes people uncomfortable.

The YouTube video shows an atheist going out in public and trying to talk people out of superstitious and spiritual beliefs. In this particular clip, the atheist approaches and talks with a Christian woman walking on a trail. Unaware of what he is trying to do, she thinks the conversation is an interview and completely misses an opportunity to share her faith.

She answers the atheist's questions and tries to explain her own beliefs, but in our observation, she is not careful to think about how the interviewer, or people who watch the video, may interpret what she is saying. For instance, when pressed about whether a sincere Hindu can get into heaven, it sounds as if she says people can go to heaven no matter what they believe. However, what she is trying to convey is that people are free to have their own beliefs and should not be forced into a particular view.

A short time later she says that Jesus is the only way. At one point she says, "Well I know it [Christianity] is true because the Holy Spirit came down and lives inside of me." Though her comment about the Holy Spirit living inside her is true, it is not helpful for the non-Christian who does not understand what that means. For that statement to be understood and not sound strange, the hearer must already have a good understanding of Christian theology.

She may wish to change her wording to better connect with listeners who do not understand Christian terminology, what we call "Christianese." If she chooses to talk about the Holy Spirit, she will need to share a lot more context and explanation to help the listener understand Christian doctrines.

Write down some common Christian words or phrases that may be misunderstood by someone who does not regularly attend church. Discuss them in your group.

Show Genuine Interest

You have likely heard the phrase, "People don't care what you know until they know that you care." This is a great principle. We never want someone to think that they are just a notch on our evangelism belt. Rather, we want to demonstrate genuine concern for their well-being.

At the same time, this can be taken too far. Some Christians don't think they can share their faith or the Gospel until they have established a deep relationship with someone, but that is not realistic in many situations. While we need to show people with whom we interact that we care about them, what that looks like will be unique to each situation. For instance, how we interact with the person next to us on an airplane will be different than how we interact with a neighbor or a family member.

The person at the check-out counter at the store	Someone you sit next to on an airplane	A co-worker	A family member

(Think of some ways you could show genuine interest and care for the person in these situations.)

Know The Person You Are Talking With

Remember that in the last lesson we learned Peter and Paul met their audience on common ground. In order to meet a person on common ground, it's helpful to find out about some of their experiences and their worldview. We may be limited in what we're able to learn based on the situation, but by showing interest and asking questions, we can find out a lot. Some helpful things to ask about include:

Personal Story and Experience

Everyone has a personal story, a journey that is unique to them. People also have some sort of religious experience or belief about ultimate reality that is informed by their life experiences.

Worldview

Everyone has a worldview, an overarching view of reality and the world that determines how they understand themselves, God, and the world. We can discover a person's worldview by how they answer the big questions about life, like those listed on the next page.

Fill in the blank beside each question that identifies each of the five main topics comprising a person's worldview (Meaning, Origin, Destiny, Identity, Morality)

M_______________ :What codes do they follow for right and wrong? Who determines right and wrong?

O_______________ :Where do they think the universe came from? Living things? Humans?

I _______________ :How would they answer, "What is a human?"
(E.g., What do they think humans are? Products of evolution, animals, uniquely created?)

M_______________ :Is there a purpose or meaning to human living? If so, what do they think it is?

D _______________ :What do they think happens to a human who dies? Do they think there is an afterlife?

Look For Opportunities To Be On Their Side

Often when talking with someone who is not a Christian, we can end up focusing on the differences between their views and Christianity, which can turn the conversation into an "us vs. them" debate. This is not an effective tactic. Instead, we can think of what we've learned about the person and find areas where we can disagree with something they disagree with or agree with something they agree with.

When the non-Christian said "I just really hate how Christianity is all about following rules, but the Christians I knew were total hypocrites," most of us as Christians would be tempted to respond defensively.

Read the following possible responses. Place a check mark beside the response(s) below that would be most characteristic of you had you not learned a more effective way to respond:

- ☐ I think you are generalizing since many Christians are not hypocrites.
- ☐ I know many Christians who are not hypocrites.
- ☐ Well, you are a hypocrite, too.
- ☐ There are hypocrites in every religion.
- ☐ Well, you are wrong that Christianity is all about rules.
- ☐ Other: ________________________________

. . .

If you pay attention, you will see opportunities like this in many conversations with non-Christians. There is certainly a time to defend certain beliefs, practices, etc.

Very often though, what a person is rejecting as Christianity is not Jesus and a Gospel-centered Christianity but instead an inaccurate message, such as the false or confused gospels we considered in Session 3.

This is part of the spiritual warfare we spoke about in lesson 1. Remember that Christianity is based on the death and resurrection of Jesus, not on how many rules we can follow.

. . .

Remember That Jesus Is Right, Not Us

One concern for many Christians is to appear non-judgmental. We may feel trapped by someone implying that we ourselves are condemning anyone who thinks differently than us. It can appear that we have determined ultimate truth which applies to everyone else as well.

Consider this small segment (presented by Whirl D Vue and Reese Zerve) from a conversation one of our team members had with a man who was raised in a large, traditional Christian denomination but is now a Universalist (believing there is a heaven and everyone goes there, no matter what).

The conversation began with our team member being asked about his work and him explaining the basic idea of Engage 360.

The conversation continued with the Universalist asking about how we could know what Jesus said and whether we can trust the Bible.

SO THEN YOU'RE ONE OF THOSE PEOPLE WHO THINK THAT ONLY CHRISTIANS CAN GO TO HEAVEN? I USED TO BE LIKE THAT. BUT YOU'RE WRONG, AND TOO NARROW MINDED. PEOPLE DON'T HAVE TO WORRY. EVERYONE WILL GO TO HEAVEN.

THAT IS AN INTERESTING SHIFT IN THE CONVERSATION. WHAT IS THE BASIS ON WHICH YOU DETERMINED EVERYONE WILL GO TO HEAVEN?

IT IS JUST TOO NARROW TO THINK OTHERWISE. PEOPLE DON'T NEED TO WORRY. IT'S NO DIFFERENT THAN YOU SAYING ONLY SOME PEOPLE GO TO HEAVEN.

I THINK THAT IS WHERE THERE WOULD BE A DIFFERENCE BETWEEN US. IT SEEMS LIKE YOU ARE SAYING THAT YOU DETERMINED ON YOUR OWN WHAT WILL HAPPEN TO EVERYONE AFTER THEY DIE. I AM SAYING THAT I HAVE NO WAY OF KNOWING THAT KIND OF THING DIRECTLY, WHICH IS WHY I TRUST WHAT JESUS SAYS ABOUT WHAT HAPPENS AFTER WE DIE.

JESUS PROVED HE WAS GOD THROUGH THE MIRACLES HE PERFORMED AND MOST IMPORTANTLY BY RISING FROM THE DEAD. THAT IS WHY I CAN CONFIDENTLY SAY THAT ONLY JESUS KNOWS, AND I CAN FULLY TRUST HIM BECAUSE HE HAS GIVEN US REASONS TO DO SO.

We will discuss how to respond to those questions in the next session. But notice how the Universalist was presenting it as though the Christian could not say for sure that only some people went to heaven, but he was comfortable claiming that everyone would go to heaven.

Once he was asked to explain his rationale it became clear the Universalist had no evidence for his claim other than the fact he did not like the idea of a narrow religion that did not "allow" everyone to go to heaven.

Our team member presented the need for a solid basis upon which to make such a strong claim and presented Jesus as the only authority who would know for sure what happens. Jesus is the authority not us. Jesus is the one who is right about heaven, not individual Christians.

Remember back to our definition of faith in Session 2 being, "A belief based on authority in which one actively trusts." Be sure that in your conversations you make clear it is Jesus that the person needs to believe or reject, not you, and then give them reasons to trust Jesus.

Ask Three Questions When Presented With A Challenge

Asking good questions is one of the most important principles you can learn to be effective in spiritual conversations. While we encourage taking time to get to know a person and finding common ground, the intent is to use this as a bridge to having the opportunity to share the Gospel. At some point, you will likely be asked a question or have objections raised against Christianity. Your initial reaction may be to immediately answer to defend Christianity or to try to avoid the question altogether. We suggest a third option:

...

Here are 3 questions that can be used to respond to almost any question or objection raised against Christianity. You will see them below in their simplest form and then we will go into more depth on each question.

- Where did you hear that?
- How do you know that it is true?
- What does it matter?

...

Question 1
Where Did You Hear That?

When someone makes a claim or raises an objection, it can be useful to know the source of the information behind it. Once we know the source, we can choose to respond directly to it, offer to investigate it ourselves, or give a recommendation where the other person can find relevant information about it.

Using the information in the above paragraph, list below three responses available to us once we know the source of the non-Christian's claim

1. R ______________________________

2. O ______________________________

3. G ______________________________

(A few examples of conversations our team has had will follow with some help from our cast members.)

Dialogue 1

WELL YOU KNOW JESUS WAS ACTUALLY MARRIED, RIGHT?

THAT'S AN INTERESTING CLAIM. WHERE DID YOU HEAR THAT?

I THINK IT WAS A SHOW ON TV.

DO YOU REMEMBER WHICH ONE?

NO, I DON'T?

Dialogue 2

WHILE THE BIBLE IS HELPFUL THERE ARE A LOT OF CHANGES THAT HAVE BEEN MADE OVER TIME.

I WAS NOT AWARE OF THAT. WHERE DID YOU HEAR THAT?

WELL IT STARTED OUT PURE BUT ONCE THE APOSTLES DIED THE CHURCH WAS CORRUPTED AND THE BIBLE STARTED TO BE CHANGED.

THAT WOULD BE PRETTY SIGNIFICANT IF TRUE. BUT WHERE DID YOU SPECIFICALLY HEAR THOSE CLAIMS?

WELL WE HAVE LEARNED ABOUT IT THROUGH TEACHING FROM THE LEADERS AND MATERIALS FROM OUR CHURCH.

THAT WOULD BE AN INTERESTING TOPIC TO STUDY TOGETHER. WHY DON'T YOU COME TO OUR HOUSE NEXT WEEK AND BRING SOME MATERIALS THAT DOCUMENT THE CHANGES YOU MENTIONED, AND I WILL DO SOME RESEARCH AS WELL. IT SHOULD BE A HELPFUL CONVERSATION FOR BOTH OF US.

In the three dialogues, which of the three helpful responses did the Christians give?

1. ______________________________

2. ______________________________

3. ______________________________

Dialogue 3

WE DON'T EVEN KNOW IF JESUS WAS REAL. THEY JUST USED HIM TO GET RICH AND HAVE POWER OVER ALL THOSE PEOPLE.

WHERE DID YOU HEAR THAT THE FIRST CHRISTIANS GOT RICH AND POWERFUL?

I DON'T REMEMBER.

HAVE YOU EVER READ ANYTHING ABOUT THE FIRST CHRISTIANS?

I DON'T THINK SO.

YOU SHOULD TAKE TIME TO READ ABOUT IT. IT IS QUITE FASCINATING HOW THEY WERE WILLING TO GIVE UP MUCH OF WHAT THEY HAD AND MANY WERE EVEN WILLING TO DIE. THERE WAS NOT WEALTH AND POWER ASSOCIATED WITH CHRISTIANITY UNTIL HUNDREDS OF YEARS AFTER JESUS WAS ON EARTH. I COULD GET YOU A BOOK TO READ THAT TALKS ABOUT THE BEGINNING OF CHRISTIANITY. WOULD YOU LIKE TO READ IT?

Question 2
How do you know that is true?

This question can follow up a discussion of "Where did you hear that?" or can be asked on its own. This question is meant to facilitate a discussion about how we would find out if any given claim is true. While it is important to look at the credibility of a source of information ("Where did you hear that"), we need to also remember that what someone might consider a "good" or expert source can still be wrong, and a "bad" or amateur source can be right.

It is usually wise to give more weight to an expert source, but we must always be aware that even experts can be wrong and often disagree with one another. Asking a question along the lines of "How do you know that is true?" will help to assess how seriously the person we are speaking with has thought through their claim. Then we can decide how seriously we should pursue a discussion or further study of the claim.

Try reading out loud the dialogues on the previous page out loud in order to hear yourself saying them. Then, put your study guide down and let the other person read the non-Christian's lines. Try to give the response in your own words, without looking. Your partner can prompt you, as needed. This exercise will increase your confidence so that you will be able to offer the response in an actual conversation!

Dialogue 1

I SAW A SHOW THAT SAID THERE WERE GOSPELS THAT DIDN'T GET INCLUDED IN THE BIBLE THAT SHOULD HAVE, AND THOSE GOSPELS ARE DIFFERENT THAN WHAT YOU READ IN THE BIBLE TODAY.

I HAVE HEARD CLAIMS LIKE THAT BUT NEVER REALLY HAD A GOOD REASON TO LOOK INTO THEM. DO YOU KNOW HOW WE COULD FIND OUT WHICH GOSPELS ARE THE GENUINE ONES AND WHICH ARE MADE UP?

I CAN'T REMEMBER THE NAME OF THE SHOW AS IT WAS A WHILE AGO, PROBABLY ON THE HISTORY CHANNEL OR SOMETHING LIKE THAT.

I THINK I COULD FIND SOMEONE WHO KNOWS WHERE TO FIND INFORMATION ON THIS TOPIC. LET'S GET TOGETHER NEXT WEEK AND I WILL LET YOU KNOW WHAT I FIND.

Dialogue 2

SO, DO YOU THINK THAT ONLY CHRISTIANS GO TO HEAVEN?

YES.

YOU DON'T NEED TO BURDEN YOURSELF WITH ALL THAT. EVERYONE WILL GO TO HEAVEN.

HOW DO YOU KNOW THAT IS TRUE?

IT JUST IS TRUE.

SO, YOU THINK THAT YOU ARE THE EXPERT ON KNOWING WHAT HAPPENS TO PEOPLE AFTER THEY DIE?

WELL YOU ARE DOING THE SAME THING.

I CAN SEE HOW YOU MIGHT THINK THAT. THE DIFFERENCE IS YOU ARE SAYING YOUR BELIEF IS TRUE BECAUSE YOU HOLD IT. I AM SAYING JESUS IS THE EXPERT ON WHAT HAPPENS TO PEOPLE AFTER THEY DIE BECAUSE HE ROSE FROM THE DEAD. HAS ANYONE TOLD YOU ABOUT EVIDENCE FOR THE RESURRECTION?

Question 3
What does it matter?

This question can help both you and the person you are talking with make the most important assessment of all: even if the claim is true, what does it matter? What we are trying to understand is what the implications are of a given claim for the truth of Christianity and the Gospel.

There are at least two ways we need to think about a claim when asking this question. First, we need to be aware that the person making the claim or objection to Christianity may have a personal experience (perhaps a painful one) tied to the objection. This means we need to be sensitive to them because a really bad reason logically can still feel like a really good reason emotionally. We may need to connect with them as a friend and "be on their side," agreeing with them that the painful experience is really bad. Second, we need to assess if the claim affects whether Christianity is true.

Dialogue 1

(Personal Connection Needed First)

CHRISTIANS ARE HYPOCRITES WHO THINK THEY ARE BETTER THAN EVERYONE ELSE.

WHAT MAKES YOU SAY THAT? DID YOU GROW UP GOING TO CHURCH?

YES, BUT LEFT WHEN I WENT TO COLLEGE. MOST OF THEM WERE JUDGMENTAL AND HATEFUL.

WOW. THAT SOUNDS PRETTY TERRIBLE. WHAT HAPPENED?

MY DAD ACTED LIKE A GREAT CHRISTIAN AT CHURCH BUT AT HOME HE TREATED MY MOM TERRIBLY. WHEN HE DIVORCED HER, OUR CHURCH FRIENDS SHUNNED US.

I AM REALLY SORRY YOU HAD TO GO THROUGH THAT! CHRISTIANS CAN BE QUITE A MESS. I AM WITH YOU IN REJECTING THAT KIND OF BEHAVIOR. IF YOUR CHURCH FRIENDS HAD BEEN FOLLOWING JESUS'S EXAMPLE, THEY WOULD HAVE LOOKED FOR WAYS TO HELP YOUR FAMILY. HOW IS YOUR RELATIONSHIP WITH YOUR PARENTS TODAY?

A BIT BETTER, BUT THEY STILL DON'T TALK TO EACH OTHER MUCH.

IT IS NOT ALWAYS EASY TO BE A CHRISTIAN WHEN I SEE WHAT GOES ON. I REMIND MYSELF THAT I AM A CHRISTIAN NOT BECAUSE OF THE PEOPLE AROUND ME BUT BECAUSE I AM CONVINCED JESUS WAS ACTUALLY RAISED FROM THE DEAD. I WOULD ENCOURAGE YOU TO LOOK AGAIN AT THE LIFE OF JESUS.

From memory, write below the 3 questions that we need to ask when someone raises a question or objection about Christianity

1. Where ____?

2. How ____?

3. What ____?

...

While we are preparing to ask people these questions in our conversations with them, we need to be prepared to answer those same kinds of questions ourselves. If we are going to tell people, "Jesus is the way," then we should be prepared for them to ask us, "Why is He the way, and how do you know that is true?"
In the final lesson, we will take steps to prepare for just these kinds of questions.

...

CHALLENGE

Ask 3 people about their spiritual background and how that has shaped them into who they are today.

- Look for opportunities to discuss Christianity and be looking for opportunities to be on their side in rejecting bad or false forms of Christianity. After identifying with them, take the time to explain the core of Christianity,

Baby Step Challenge

Ask 1 person about their spiritual background and how that has shaped them into who they are today. This can be someone you know.

Prayer

Lord, thank You that You have done everything necessary for our salvation, and offered it as a free gift to all who trust in You. Please help me remember the Gospel is not about what I have done, but what You have done. Help me to keep that message simple and clear, remembering it is the work of Your Holy Spirit to save, not mine. Help me to lovingly walk with people, always pointing them to Jesus so they can come to understand how much You love them. Amen

Now I Know!

How To Have Spiritual Conversations

...

Seven keys to initiating and guiding spiritual conversations:

- TALK; don't preach.
- GUARD your conversation as a "No Christianese" zone.
- SHOW genuine interest.
- KNOW the person you are talking with.
- LOOK for opportunities to be on "their side."
- REMEMBER that Jesus is right, not us.
- ASK three questions when presented with a challenge.
  - Where did you hear that?
  - How do you know that is true?
  - What does it matter?

...

Find additional Session 5 resources at www.E360m.org/eywresources

Session 6

How We Can Know Christianity Is True

Paul, a servant of Christ Jesus, called to be an apostle, set apart for the gospel of God, which he promised beforehand through his prophets in the holy Scriptures, concerning his son, who was descended from David according to the flesh and was declared to be the Son of God in power according to the Spirit of holiness by his resurrection from the dead, Jesus Christ our Lord.

–Romans 1:1-4

...

Given that we believe a biblical approach to sharing our faith involves talking with people about what they believe and why then it is also reasonable for us to expect to be asked the same kinds of questions. When we share the gospel message, it is reasonable for non-Christians to ask us questions about how and why we came to believe in Jesus. Specifically, they may ask:

- Why Jesus?
- How do we know Jesus rose from the dead?
- What if the apostles made everything up?
- What if the Bible has been changed over time?

Some Christians have thought through all of these questions, and more, about the Christian faith, while others may have never considered anything beyond their own personal Christian experience. No matter our background, we all have room to grow in our knowledge of the evidence that support our faith.

...

Five Tips for Learning Evidences for the Christian faith

The great news is that there is plenty of evidence that Christianity is true. We are going to share some of the most significant evidences in this lesson. As we do, let's remember several tips for learning the evidences for the Christian faith:

You Are Your Own Measuring Stick

Focus on growing in your own skills, not comparing yourself to others who know more.

Focus On One Thing At A Time

You don't have to learn everything at once. Start with one question or topic to focus on, then study and ponder that one topic. See our chart on p. 119 to help guide you through the most essential questions and topics to learn first.

Keep On Keeping On

We often get mentally tired and are tempted to quit when the information seems to be too much or too hard, especially when questions arise out of our study or things seem unclear.

The reward of working through hard questions is increased knowledge of and love for the infinite God and increased confidence in sharing the truth of the Gospel with others.

Get Comfortable With Not Knowing All The Answers

When you don't know the answer to a question, you can say, "I don't know, that is a good question. Let me look into it and get back to you."

Identify And Use Your Resources

No one is an expert in everything. Your church or even your group is filled with people with diverse backgrounds, personalities, abilities, and expertise. Lean on one another.

Also, when a topic falls outside your interest or aptitude, you can be sure there is a Christian expert who has written or spoken on the topic. Online resources are plentiful. We are available to help point you in the right direction!

On the lines below, write the five tips for learning the evidences for the Christian faith. Place a star beside the one that you think will be most difficult for you to do. Ask the Lord to enable you to do all that He is asking you to do.

____

____

____

____

____

Answering Four Essential Questions about the Christian faith

With these tips in mind let's explore the most essential questions that every Christian needs to know how to answer. The chart on the next page is a helpful guide.

I UNDERSTAND YOU ARE A CHRISTIAN AND YOU THINK JESUS IS THE WAY TO HEAVEN, BUT THERE ARE SO MANY RELIGIONS OUT THERE. HOW DO YOU KNOW JESUS IS ACTUALLY THE WAY?

Why Jesus?

____

____

____

____

____

____

____

(Write down how you would respond to someone who asked you this question.)

How We Can Know Christianity Is True

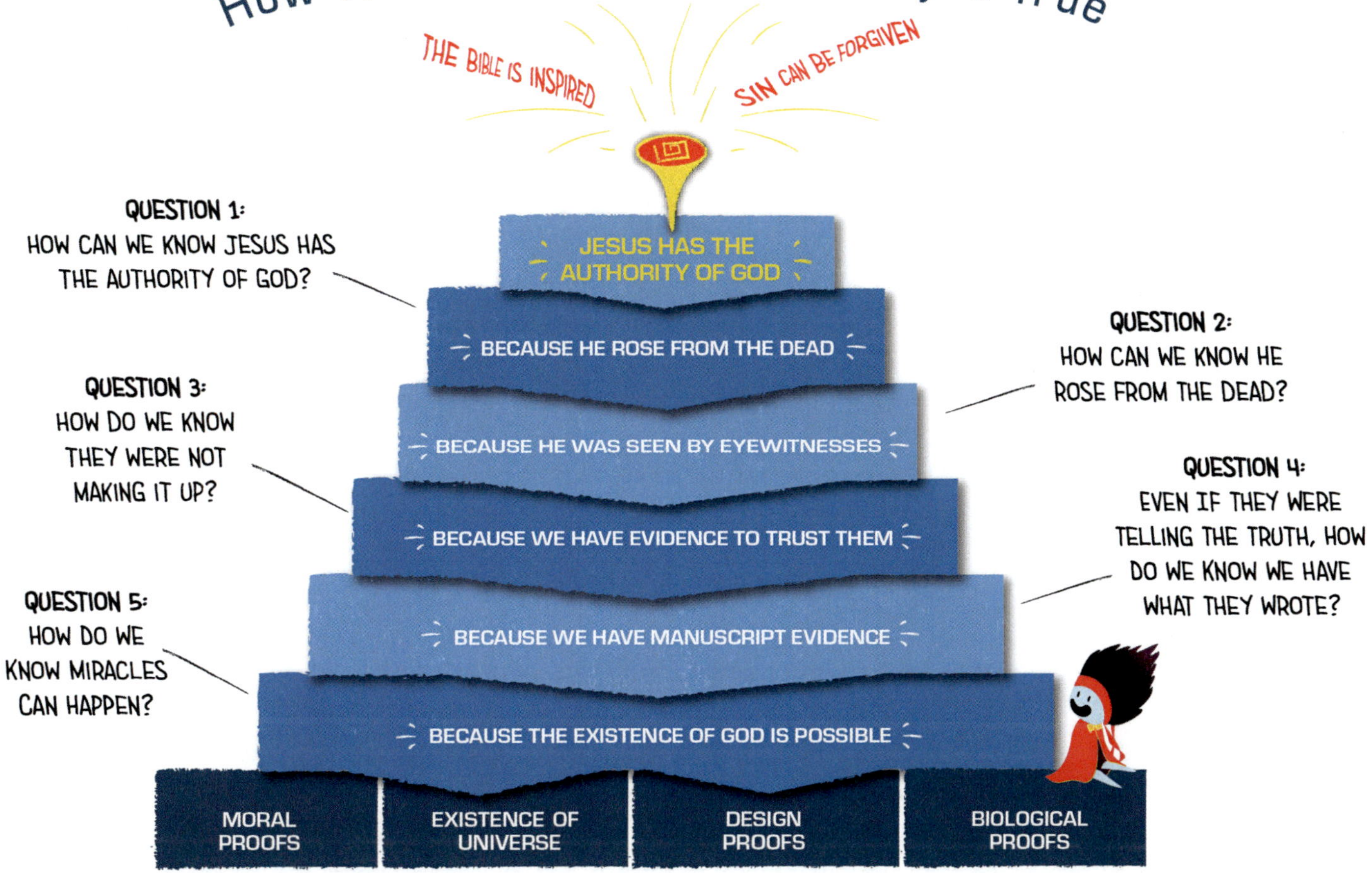

If Jesus has the authority of God then the Bible is inspired and sin can be forgiven. How do we know Jesus has the authority of God? Follow the questions and answers on this chart.

The apostles in the New Testament were certainly aware of the need to answer this question, not only for the Gentiles but also for their fellow Jews. Imagine the complications of saying you still worship the One True God but then seemingly denying a core tenet of Judaism that God is One by claiming a man to be equal with God! Yet this is the truth, and we need to be prepared to defend it just as Peter, Paul, and many other early church leaders were.

When we talk with someone about our reasons for believing in Jesus, what we are not saying is, I have personally determined that Jesus is the way to heaven. It is Jesus who is making the claim and in whom we are trusting, not ourselves. This is the subtle but significant point Reese Zerve makes in answer to S.K. Eptic's question.

How Can We Know Jesus Has The Authority Of God?

Remembering our previous lessons on the Gospel and biblical evangelism, what was the single event to which Peter and Paul appealed as proof that Jesus was the way? The ______________________

Since faith entails believing something based on our trust in an authority, when we act on faith, we must ask why we trust our specific authority. For Paul, the truth of Christianity and all of Jesus's claims hinged on the resurrection. The resurrection establishes that Jesus is the ultimate authority and speaks as God.

Take a few minutes to read 1 Corinthians 15. As you read through the chapter, complete the following sentences in this passage to show that Paul considered the resurrection to be the central truth of the Christian faith.

v. 3-4: He says that Jesus' death for our sins, His burial, and His resurrection of Christ are of "____________________ importance."

v. 14: He says that if Christ has not been raised, then "our ____________________ is in vain and your ________________ is in vain."

v. 15: He says if Christ has not been raised then "we are even found to be __________________ God, because we testified about God that he ______________________ Christ."

v. 17: He says "If Christ has not been raised, "your faith is ________________________ and you are still in your _____________."

v. 18: He says that if Christ has not been raised, "then those also who have fallen asleep in Christ have ______________________________."

v. 22: He contrasts Christ with Adam, saying that in Adam "all _____," so also in Christ shall all be made ________________," pointing out that just as Christ lived again, so will we.

v. 42-44: He promises that what happened to Christ's body will also happen to the bodies of believers, saying, "What is sown is perishable; what is raised is ______________________. It is sown in dishonor; it is raised in ______________________. It is sown a natural body: it is raised a ________________________ body."

How Can We Know Jesus Rose From The Dead?

Imagine you are in the same conversation as before and the person says, "Okay, fine. If Jesus rose from the dead that would be a big deal and make me think a bit more about Christianity. But how could you possibly know that Jesus really died and rose from the dead?"

____

____

____

____

(Write down how you would respond if someone asked you the question above)

It is not uncommon for Christians and non-Christians to think that believing Jesus rose from the dead is a matter of faith, and by faith they mean something along the lines of believing in something you do not have evidence for. However, the Bible paints a very different picture. The Christian faith is reasonable; we have good reasons to trust in the authority of Jesus . On that basis, we believe what He says about things we cannot directly know on our own.

Consulting 1 Corinthians 15:3-8, fill in the blanks below to show how Paul provides evidence for the resurrection as a fact.

v.3: that Christ ______________ for our sins in ______________________ with the ______________________,

v.4: that he was _______________, that he was __________________ on the third day in __________________ with the __________________,

v.5: and that he _______________________ to Cephas, then to the twelve.

v.6: Then he ______________________ to more than five hundred brothers at one time, most of whom are still ______________________, though some have fallen asleep.

v.7: Then he _______________ to James, then to all the apostles

v.8: Last of all, as to one untimely born, he ________________ also to me.

- What phrase does Paul repeat as evidence that Christ's death and resurrection were prophesied throughout the Scriptures (the Old Testament)? "in ___________________ with the ____________________"
- How many times does Paul use the word "appeared" in order to emphasize that the claim of Christ's resurrection from the dead was supported by His multiple physical appearances to hundreds of believers after the event? ____________________

Why do you think Paul mentioned that most of those to whom Christ appeared were still alive?

In John 1:1-4 below, underline the words that describe how the eyewitnesses verified the reality of the resurrection through their human senses:

John 1:1-4

1 That which was from the beginning, which we
have heard, which we have seen with our eyes,
which we looked upon and have touched with our
hands, concerning the word of life— 2 the life was
made manifest, and we have seen it, and testify to
it and proclaim to you the eternal life, which was
with the Father and was made manifest to us— 3
that which we have seen and heard we proclaim
also to you, so that you too may have fellowship
with us; and indeed our fellowship is with the
Father and with his Son Jesus Christ. 4 And we
are writing these things so that our joy may be
complete.

Faith in Jesus involves trusting that Jesus can forgive sin and that He is the way to God, but it is not blind faith. We know Jesus rose from the dead because there were hundreds of eyewitnesses who saw Jesus alive after the crucifixion.

This happened at different times, in different places, and with different groups of people. They actually saw Him killed and then risen from the dead; this is the reason so many were willing to die for following Jesus as the Christ.

But What If They Made It All Up?

We have established that Jesus reveals His authority to forgive sin and that He is the way to God through His miracles (namely, the resurrection), and we know He was raised because there were hundreds of eyewitnesses.

However, the savvy seeker or skeptic might then say, "Well, all of the sources you are relying on are from the people who started Christianity, and they could have made the whole thing up."

If you are a Christian, most likely, you think other religions are merely the creation of humans to explain the world around them, or in some cases, a means of gaining power over others. However, we as Christians don't get a free pass.

The Christian needs to be able to explain what separates Christianity from other religions. When we are on college campuses, we hear a lot of different ideas from people about Christianity being made up.

Sometimes they will even compare it to other religions. If we are going to trust the eyewitness testimony of the apostles, then we will need to be able to explain why we can trust them.

You may have concluded that most of the apostles and many early Christians died for what they were teaching. However, you may run across someone who says, "Well, it certainly shows us they were committed if they died for their religion, but the people who carried out the 9/11 attacks were also committed to their religion." Their point is well made. Being sincere and zealous enough to die for one's belief does not prove that the belief is true; it only proves that they sincerely believe it is true.

Compare the basis of the first-century apostles' beliefs and those of the 9/11 Muslim terrorists. In light of each of their sources for their belief, what is a major difference between the apostles and the 9/11 attackers?

____

____

Though you may have come up with several differences, the one significant difference is that the apostles were the eyewitnesses to the events they describe, whereas the 9/11 attackers were following teachings from religious leaders over 1,000 years after their religion was started.

This does not mean they were insincere, but rather that they did not have first-hand knowledge that their religion is true. But the apostles were eyewitnesses to the actual events and they knew whether it was true or false.

People of many religions have been, and still are, martyred for a faith that they believe is true. However, if the apostles made up their claims about Christ and His resurrection, then they willingly suffered and died for a faith that they knew all along was a lie. This does not make sense. Nor is it reasonable to think that they made up Christianity in order to gain wealth and power. They were not like some denominations in history, with buildings all over the world and wielding influence over high-level political leaders.

Instead, history records that they were beaten, jailed, and hated by their own people. Yet because they knew that Jesus really had died, was buried, and physically rose back to life, the apostles who themselves recorded their fearful hiding from authorities after Jesus's death became bold, courageous witnesses to the events they themselves had witnessed: that Jesus died for sin, arose from the grave, and therefore, only in Him could one have eternal life with God. Have you ever reflected on the sacrifice the early Christians made?

Take a minute to consider this fact and thank God that He sustained so many even in the face of death. If you have not read stories of early and recent Christian martyrs, we would encourage you to do so. One great resource is Foxe's Book of Martyrs.

What If The Bible Has Been Changed Over Time?

We have established Jesus has the authority to forgive sin and that He proved to be the only way to God because He rose from the dead. We know He rose from the dead because of the eyewitness testimony of the apostles. And we know the apostles were firsthand witnesses who were willing to suffer and die for what they saw and believed. Where do we learn about the apostles' eye-witness accounts?
In the _______________.

The Bible contains an incredible collection of writings from the apostles. However, not everyone accepts the Bible as what Christians claim it to be. The more conversations you have, the more likely it is that someone like S.K. Eptic will bring up objections to the truth of the Bible.

How would you respond if S.K. Eptic made this claim to you?

THE PROBLEM IS THAT YOU ARE BASING ALL OF THIS ABOUT JESUS AND HIS FOLLOWERS FROM THE BIBLE, BUT THAT IS THOUSANDS OF YEARS OLD AND HAS BEEN CHANGED SO MUCH OVER TIME. IT KEPT GETTING TRANSLATED FROM ONE LANGUAGE TO ANOTHER, AND DIFFERENT PEOPLE HAVE USED IT FOR THEIR OWN POWER AND PURPOSES. AT THIS POINT WE HAVE NO IDEA WHAT THE FIRST FOLLOWERS OF JESUS SAID OR IF THEY EVEN EXISTED.

Many Christian would struggle to give a concise response to this challenge, but applying our "3 questions" from the last lesson could be a good start, especially since SK has made several specific assertions.

- Where did the person hear that there were so many changes?
- Could they show you the changes that were made?
- Even if they could show changes or errors in a translation, what would the implication be?

One of our team members, Matt, really struggled with this question when he was a skeptic and not following any religion. He asked Christians how they got the Bible in their hand and how they knew it said roughly the same thing as what was written 2,000 years ago. Sadly, not a single Christian was able to answer this question for him, but later he learned it is really quite simple.

...

What do we mean by an "early" manuscript?

Manuscripts are ancient handwritten copies of the New Testament or fragments of it, in Greek or other ancient languages.

To say that a manuscript is early means that it was written close to the time of the original. One of the earliest New Testament fragments is the John Ryland's manuscript, a small fragment from John 8 that has been dated to within about 30 years of when the Apostle John lived.

In 2002, Dr. Daniel B. Wallace founded the Center for the Study of New Testament Manuscripts (CSNTM) and through the use of technology, has preserved images of hundreds of thousands of Greek New Testament manuscripts.

You can view images of these manuscripts at their online site. http://www.csntm.org/About/WhoWeAre

...

I'VE HEARD THAT BIBLICAL TRANSMISSION IS LIKE A GAME OF TELEPHONE, WHERE PEOPLE SIT IN A CIRCLE AND START A MESSAGE WITH ONE PERSON WHO WHISPERS WHAT THEY HEAR TO THE NEXT PERSON AND SO ON, AND THEY HEAR HOW THE MESSAGE ENDS UP CHANGING BY THE TIME IT REACHES THE LAST PERSON IN THE CIRCLE.

...

However, that is not how we got the Bible that we use today. It is not a translation of a translation of a translation of a translation. Instead, experts in the original languages are translating directly from early manuscripts into modern languages.

...

Comparing the ancient manuscripts, textual critics reconstruct the New Testament to a high level of accuracy. Most differences of wording and spelling among ancient manuscripts are insignificant. Of those that do affect meaning, none affects a central doctrine of the Christian faith.

While there can be some minor subtleties lost in the process, the core message is not affected. This is further strengthened by the immense manuscript evidence that we have for the New Testament.

Additional resources are available if you are interested in a deeper dive on this topic. The big picture is that given the abundance of manuscript evidence, Christians are in a good position to say with confidence that the Bible we read today is a faithful translation of the very words of Jesus, Peter, Paul, and other figures from the early Church.

CHECK OUT ADDITIONAL RESOURCES ABOUT BIBLICAL RELIABILITY AT WWW.E360M.ORG/EYWRESOURCES!

CHALLENGE

Ask 3 people if they have ever had someone explain to them the evidence behind why a Christian would believe Jesus? If they have heard evidence before, ask them what kind of evidence and how it influenced their belief in who Jesus Christ is.

If they have not heard evidence behind why a Christian would believe in Jesus, walk them through the conversation chart, making sure to meet them where they are by paying attention to what they know about each area of evidence we have just covered.

Baby Step Challenge

Ask 1 person if they have ever had someone explain to them the evidence behind why a Christian would believe Jesus. Take the conversation as far as you are comfortable.

PRAYER

Lord, thank You for helping me understand the truth of the Gospel. As I try to communicate that truth to others, please help me work through my limitations by relying totally upon You. Help me not to compare myself to others, but to be confident in what I have learned, knowing that I too am continuing to grow in my faith. In all that I do and say, please help me to always reflect Jesus to others. Amen

Now I Know!

How Can I Know Christianity Is True?

Five tips for learning evidences for the Christian faith:

- Remember, you are your own measuring stick.
- Focus on one thing at a time.
- Keep on keeping on.
- Get comfortable with not knowing all the answers.
- Identify and use resources.

How to answer four essential questions about the Christian faith:

- **Why Jesus?**
  We believe in Jesus because there is strong evidence that He really rose from the dead.
- **How do we know Jesus rose from the dead?**
  We can be confident because there were hundreds of eyewitnesses.
- **What if the apostles made everything up?**
  This is unlikely since they had nothing to gain and were martyred for their faith.
- **What if the Bible has been changed over time?**
  The manuscripts (handwritten copies) we do have can be compared to reconstruct what the originals said. We can reconstruct the original words of the New Testament to a high level of accuracy.

Find additional Session 6 resources at www.E360m.org/eywresources

Evangelism Survey (Follow-up)

Date: ____________

1	2	3	4	5
Need Practice		Making Progress		Confident/ Comfortable

- **How comfortable are you starting a spiritual conversation?** ____________
  (On a scale of 1 to 5, with 5 being "Comfortable" and 1 being "Not very comfortable", write down the number.)

- **Once started, how comfortable are you guiding a spiritual conversation?** ____________
  (On a scale of 1 to 5, with 5 being "Comfortable" and 1 being "Not very comfortable", write down the number.)

- **How confidently can you explain the Gospel to someone?** ____________
  (On a scale of 1 to 5, with 5 being "Comfortable" and 1 being "Not very comfortable", write down the number.)

- **How often do you have spiritual conversations with others?** (Circle the word that best describes where you are.)

  Daily **Weekly** **Monthly** **Rarely** **Never**

Please fill out the survey again now that you have completed the last session.
Please enter your results from both surveys at www.E360m.org/EYWsurvey.com.

Made in the USA
Las Vegas, NV
02 May 2025

21272147R10081